Observations on

ADOLESCENCE

The Third Phase of Human Development

by

Rudolf Steiner

Published by:
The Association of Waldorf Schools of North America
3911 Bannister Road
Fair Oaks, CA 95628

Observations on
ADOLESCENCE
The Third Phase of Human Development

Author: Rudolf Steiner

Great Britain Editor: Christopher Clouder

North American Editor: David Mitchell,
in conjunction with the AWSNA Waldorf
High School Research Project

Proofreaders: Nancy Jane, Ann Simpson

Cover: Hallie Wooten

© 2001 by AWSNA

ISBN # 1-888365-31-5

Table of Contents

Foreword

This book represents a collaboration which gathers together statements Rudolf Steiner said or wrote about adolescence. Throughout the years I accumulated golden nuggets of wisdom Steiner had made about adolescence which were not yet translated into English. Christopher Clouder from the Steiner Schools Fellowship in Great Britain had a collection of material he used in teacher training. Betty Staley from Rudolf Steiner College had a translation of comments Steiner made about the astral body which she used at the College. Permission was granted by Michael Dobson of the Anthroposophic Press and Sevak Gulbekian from Rudolf Steiner Press in England to use material under their respective copyrights. The collection of comments is wide ranging, and there is some redundancy, but this, in my opinion, demonstrates how Steiner approached the same topic from different perspectives.

The material speaks not only about adolescence but also about the seven to fourteen year phase leading up to adolescence. Steiner offers guidance to both class teachers and high school teachers who are working with young people before and during puberty.

The term "adolescent" is a relatively new word in the English language. It first appeared in print in England in 1481 when Mark of Erecham wrote of "a certain adolescent young man." It identified the time of life between childhood and adulthood. We observe this period of life as a time of excess and exaggeration and also as a time of intense loneliness. Rudolf Steiner referred to the onset of adolescence as a gentle sprinkling of pain that never goes away.

During this age boys are often outwardly brassy in a group, but when alone they turn inward, exploring their inner fantasies, and they often seem to live in a dark cave of emotions which they cannot explain. They need an understanding, warm mother to help them make sense of their complex feeling life.

Girls, on the other hand, can be noisy, brash, sassy, flirtatious, and moody, and they can exhibit a tremendous emotional vitality. Often possessing an inner sullenness, they are helped by the cool logic of an understanding father whose main help is through listening and sharing detached, unemotional logic!

Adolescence storms in with major body changes induced by surreptitiously oozing hormones. First, we may notice that the young man's feet rapidly outgrow his shoes, and the legs and arms dangle too far from the pant cuff or shirt sleeve. The walk becomes a strut or a rowboat-like maneuvering across the pavement. The voice changes in both sexes, most notably in the boys where it falls a full octave. The girls voice falls one tone. The larynx enlarges and the vocal cords are lengthened. The jaw often drops a bit and juts out.

The center of gravity drops from the second cervical to the sacral vertebrae. The lungs increase in size in boys and girls. From about the age of ten they start to breathe differently. The girls' breathing becomes costal and is centered at the top of the ribs, while the boys' breathing drops down to $2/3$ chest and $1/3$ diaphragm. Like young lion cubs the boys enjoy bumping into each other and exult in experiencing their own vitality.

The blood pressure increases during the teenage years, and the heart, without growing much in size, doubles in mass. All of this activity, along with secondary and primary sexual characteristics which rearrange the shape of the body, are initiated by twenty-four major and over two hundred minor hormones.

Thus, adolescence is a picture of youth diving deeply down into his and her own organism.

It is not surprising that this age, of all the developmental periods of life, requires the most empathy from teachers and parents. It is hoped that this book will kindle those feelings of empathy.

– David Mitchell
North American Editor

6

Introduction

In Yevtushenko's autobiographical poem *Zima Junction*, which tells of his return as an adult to the town he grew up in, he describes a meeting between his former self as a child and his later self as an adolescent. Childhood was time when

Life solved itself without my contributions.
I had no doubts about harmonious answers
Which could and would be given to every question.
But in time there came an unexpected change in him:
I suddenly felt this necessity
of answering these questions for myself.
So shall I go on where I started from,
Sudden complexity, self generated,
disturbed by which I started on this journey.

When his child nature then speaks to his older version, he expresses his concern because this is not a state he had ever envisioned for himself, and he reminded his own youth how heavily indebted he was to his previous condition.

So youth asked if childhood would help,
And childhood smiled and promised it would help.

In this lyrical form the poet expresses the fact the human development is based on earlier states, and any understanding of our natures must take this into account. As adults we, too, need to recreate and re-enter some elements of adolescence to rediscover and gain a clearer perspective on who we are and our motivation as adults. This especially applies

7

to educators or carergivers who wish to work with young people.

In the following passages in this book Rudolf Steiner describes this transformation from the view of spiritual science. Psychologists, doctors, and educators recognize this as a critical phase in human development, but all too often the institutions that young people attend are more concerned with their future role in society rather than the sources of such "self generated questions." Steiner attempts to look deeper at human development and explore the personal evolution of this change and its outer manifestations as those of a spiritual reality. Speaking as he was in the first two decades of the last century he does not touch upon elements of the present phenomena around adolescence. However, the insight he gives as to why these occur is as vital today as it was then. The questions around adolescence are important to everybody in our contemporary culture as they have a large and often dynamic influence in how we all live our lives. It cannot be dismissed as merely a phase that will pass in time. In fact, the turbulence should be approached with respect as a general aspect of being human and the questions thus raised as a necessary regenerative impulse for which we should feel grateful. It also should be seen in the context of what preceded it and as part of the culture within which the young person is immersed. This has educational implications, as this approach suggests that the curriculum should itself try to support these inner needs and changes rather than attempt to mold the young person to a preset path of learning goals that could be irrelevant to the sensitive and idealistic human soul at this age.

The original collection of my contribution to this book is drawn from Steiner's approximately 200 educational lectures made available by Dr. Hans Rebman for the use of his colleagues in the Stuttgart-Uhlandshöhe Waldorf School as a step towards deepening their understanding of their task as high school teachers.

As anyone who has worked seriously with these texts would testify, Rudolf Steiner's insights serve as a sound basis on which the needs and questions of this age range can be fruitfully and creatively met by educators who have taken on these areas of vocational responsibility.

– Christopher Clouder
Great Britain Editor

Yevtushenko, Yevgeny. *Selected Poems*. London: Penguin Books, 1962, pp. 24-25.

Education for Adolescents

Interest in the World

When children come to the age of puberty, it is necessary to awaken within them an extraordinarily great interest in the world outside of themselves. Through the whole way in which they are educated, they must be led to look out into the world around them and into all its laws, its course, causes and effects, into human intentions and goals, not only into human beings, but into everything, even into a piece of music, for instance. All this must be brought to them in such a way that it can resound over and over within them, so that questions about nature, about the cosmos and the entire world, about the human soul, questions of history, and riddles arise in their youthful souls.

When the astral body becomes free at puberty, forces are released which can now be used for formulating these riddles. But when these riddles of the world and its manifestations do *not* arise in young souls, then these same forces are changed into something else.

When such forces become free, and it has not been possible to awaken the most intensive interest in such world-riddles, then these energies transform themselves into what they become in most young people today. They change in two directions, two urges of an instinctive kind: first into delight in power, and second into eroticism.

Unfortunately, pedagogy does not now consider this delight in power and the eroticism of young people to be the secondary results of changes in things that, until the age of twenty or twenty-one, really ought to go in an altogether different direction, but considers them to be natural elements in the human organism at puberty. If young people are rightly educated, there should be no need whatsoever to speak about love of power and eroticism to them at this age. If such things have to be spoken about during these years, this is in itself something that smacks of illness. Our entire pedagogical art and science are becoming ill, because again and again the highest value is attributed to these questions. A high value is put upon them for no other reason than that people are powerless today and have grown more and more power-less, in the age of a materialistic world conception, to inspire true interest in the world, the world in the widest sense. . . .

When we do not have enough interest in the world around us, then we are thrown back into ourselves. Taken all in all, we have to say that if we look at the chief damages created by modern civilization, they arise primarily because people are far too concerned with themselves and do not usually spend the larger part of their leisure time in concern for the world but busy themselves with how they feel and what gives them pain . . . . And the least favorable time of life to be self-occupied in this way is during the ages between fourteen, fifteen, and twenty-one years old.

The capacity for forming judgments is blossoming at this time and should be directed toward world interrelation-ships in every field. The world must become so all-engross-ing to young people that they simply do not turn their attention away from it long enough to be constantly occupied with themselves. For, as everyone knows, as far as subjective feelings are concerned, pain only becomes greater the more we think about it. It is not the objective damage but the pain of it that increases as we think more about it. In certain respects, the very best remedy for the overcoming of pain is to bring yourself, if you can, not to think about it. Now there develops in young people just between fifteen, sixteen and twenty, twenty-one, something not altogether unlike pain. This adaptation to the conditions brought about through the freeing of the astral body from the physical is really a continual experience of gentle pain. And this kind of experience immediately makes us tend towards self-preoccupation, unless we are sufficiently directed away from it and toward the world outside ourselves.

If a teacher makes a mistake while teaching a ten- or twelve-year-old, then, as far as the mutual relationship between pupil and teacher is concerned, this does not really make such a very great difference. By this I do not mean that you should make as many mistakes as possible with children of this age. . . . The feeling for the teacher's authority will flag perhaps for a while, but such things will be forgotten comparatively quickly, in any case much sooner than certain injustices are forgotten at this age. On the other hand, when you stand in front of students between fourteen, fifteen and twenty, twenty-one, you simply must not expose your latent inadequacies and so make a fool of yourself. . . .

If a student is unable to formulate a question which he or she experiences inwardly, the teachers must be capable of doing this themselves, so that they can bring about such a formulation in class, and they must be able to satisfy the feeling that then arises in the student when the question comes to expression. For if they do not do this, then when all that is mirrored there in the souls of these young people goes over into the world of sleep, into the sleeping condition, a body of detrimental, poisonous substances is produced by the unformulated questions. These poisons are developed only during the night, just when poisons ought really to be broken down and transformed instead of created. Poisons are produced that burden the brains of the young people when they go to class, and gradually everything in them stagnates, becomes "stopped up." This must and can be avoided. But it can be avoided only if the feeling is not aroused in the students: "Now again the teacher has failed to give us the right answer. We really haven't been answered at all. We can't get a satisfying answer." Those are the latent inadequacies, the self-exposures that occur when the children have the feeling: "The teacher just isn't up to giving us the answers we need." And for this inability, the personal capacities and incapacities of the teacher are not the only determining factors, but rather the pedagogical method.

If we spend too much time pouring a mass of information over young people at this age, or if we teach in such a way that they never come to lift their doubts and questions into consciousness, then, even though we are the more objective party, we expose, even if indirectly, our latent inadequacies.

You see, the teacher must, in full consciousness, be permeated through and through with all this when dealing with the transition from the ninth to the tenth grades, for it is just with the entire transformation of the courses one gives that the pedagogy must concern itself. If we have children of six or seven, then the course is already set through the fact that they are entering school, and we do not need to understand any other relationship to life. But when we lead young people over from the ninth to the tenth grade, then we must put ourselves into quite another life condition. When this happens, the children must say to themselves: "Great thunder and lightning! What's happened to the teacher! Up to now we've thought of him as a pretty bright light who has plenty to say, but now he's beginning to talk like more than a man. Why, the whole world speaks out of him!"

And when they feel the most intensive interest in particular world questions and are put into the fortunate position of being able to impart this to other young people, then the world speaks out of them also. Out of a mood of this kind, verve *(Schwung)* must arise. Verve is what teachers must bring to young people at this age, verve which above all is directed towards imagination; for although the students are developing the capacity to make judgments, judgment is actually borne out of the powers of imagination. And if you deal with the intellect intellectually, if you are not able to deal with the intellect with a certain imagination, then you have "mis-played," and you have missed the boat with them.

Young people demand imaginative powers: you must approach them with verve, and with verve of a kind that convinces them. Skepticism is something that you may not bring to them in the first half of this life-period. The most damaging judgment for the time between fourteen, fifteen, and eighteen is one that implies in a pessimistically knowledgeable way: "This is something that cannot be known." This crushes the soul of a child or a young person. It is more possible after eighteen to pass over to what is more or less in doubt. But between fourteen and eighteen it is soul-crushing, soul-debilitating, to introduce them to a certain skepticism. The subject you deal with is much less important than not bringing this debilitating pessimism to young people.

It is important for oneself as a teacher to exercise a certain amount of self-observation and not give in to any illusions; for it is fatal if, just at this age, young people feel more clever than the teacher during class, especially in secondary matters. It should be and it can be achieved, even if not right in the first lesson, that they are so gripped by what they hear that their attention will really be diverted from all the teacher's little mannerisms. Here, too, the teacher's latent inadequacies are the most fatal.

Now, if you think, my dear friends, that neglect of these matters unloads its consequences into the channels of instinctive love of power and eroticism, then you will see from the beginning how tremendously significant it is to take the education of these young people in hand in a bold and generous way. You can much more easily make mistakes with older students, for example, with those at medical school. For what you do at this earlier age works into their later life in an extraordinarily devastating way. It works destructively, for instance, upon the relationships between people. The right kind of interest in other human beings is not possible if the right sort of world interest is not aroused in the fifteen- or sixteen-year-old. If they learn only the Kant-Laplace theory of the creation of the solar system and what one learns through astronomy and astrophysics today, if they cram into their skulls only this idea of the cosmos, then in social relationships they will be just such men and women as those of our modern civilization who, out of anti-social impulses, shout about every kind of social reform but within their souls actually bring anti-social powers to expression. I have often said that the reason people make such an outcry about social matters is because they are anti-social beings.

It cannot be said often enough that in the years between fourteen and eighteen, we must build upon the fundamentally basic moral relationship between pupil and teacher in the most careful way. And here morality is to be understood in its broadest sense: that, for instance, as teachers we call up in our soul the very deepest sense of responsibility for our task. This moral attitude must show itself in that we do not give all too much acknowledgment to this deflection toward subjectivity and one's own personality. In such matters, imponderables really pass over from teacher to pupil. Mournful teachers, unalterably morose teachers who are immensely fond of their lower selves, produce in children of just this age a mirror image of themselves, or they kindle a terrible teenage revolution. More important than any approved method is that we do not expose our latent inadequacies and that we approach the children with an attitude that is inwardly moral through and through. . . .

This sickly eroticism which has grown up—also in people's minds—to such a terrible extent appears for the most part only in city dwellers who have become teachers and doctors. And only as urban life triumphs altogether in our civilization will these things come to such a terrible—I do not want to say "blossoming" but to such a frightful—degeneracy. Naturally, we must look not at appearances but at reality. It is certainly quite unnecessary to begin to organize educational homes in the country immediately. If teachers and pupils carry these same detrimental feelings out into the country and are really permeated by urban conceptions, you can call a school a country school as long as you like, you will still have a blossoming of city life to deal with. . . .

What we have spoken about here today is of the utmost pedagogical importance and, in considering the high school years, should be taken into the most earnest consideration.

—Excerpts from a lecture given in Stuttgart on June 21, 1922. (In a few cases the repetitions appropriate for spoken style have been omitted and sentences condensed. Translated by Christy Barnes.)

Astral Body and Desire

The first part of life in which the human being develops includes the time until the child receives his second teeth. First he has the milk teeth; then he receives the second teeth. One can say the human being has the milk teeth as a result of heredity. But the second teeth he has from his ether body.

He then also has his astral body and his ego. This astral body, with the ego that is embedded in it, always desires the physical body. So we can say that the human being develops desire in his astral body. All desires are developed in the astral body.

From the receiving of the second teeth to the time of puberty, something supersensible is active in the child. And what does this supersensible something want? It gradually wants to take hold of the whole body. It is not yet there when the child has the second teeth, and it begins to receive the astral body into its entire body in such a way that it permeates the whole body. Then the child becomes more and more mature. Once the astral body has totally permeated the physical body, then the child is sexually mature. That is the important thing to know: the astral body is what brings sexual maturity into the child. . . . A person who has learned to observe clearly what it is that works its way into the body

16

during the time from the second teeth to puberty will know that this is the astral body. It gives rise to all the desires. Of course, the child already has desires before the second teeth because the astral body is embedded in the head; but later it expands throughout the entire body. You can very well observe how the astral body expands in the boy's body. The boy changes his voice and with that he also becomes sexually mature. That is the sign that the astral body has plunged into the entire physical body. In the girl you can observe it through the fact that secondary sexual organs, the breasts and so forth, develop.

You see this astral body each morning when again and again it wants to enter the physical body. For while the human being is asleep, he has no desires, neither sexual nor any other kind. The desires arise in the waking state. They arise in the morning when the astral body wants to enter the physical body. And in life this astral body craves to enter the physical body every single morning. Of course, it also wants to do this after death, but it has to get used to not being able to do this.

— GA 349/3-21-23
Lecture to the Workers

The Connection Between Breathing and Puberty

One can observe how the child, in a certain way, sleeps differently from the person she becomes after the change of teeth. The difference is not so obvious; however it exists. The child up to age seven cannot yet send into her sleeping state—into the state that the soul lives in between falling asleep and waking up—what later on it can send as soul forces; for these forces still have to do with the physical-material, that is, with the physical organism. Therefore, the child does not yet send into her sleeping state the sharply contoured concepts. The child sends into the sleep state barely contoured concepts, barely contoured mental images, but these less sharply contoured mental images have the peculiarity that they can encompass the soul-spiritual reality in a better way than the sharply contoured mental images can.

This is something important. The more sharply contoured our concepts are for the day-waking life, the less we send into the sleep state in order to grasp the realities there. That is how the child in very many cases, in fact, brings a certain knowledge of spiritual reality out of her sleep state. These sharply contoured concepts, so to say, dampen the vision for the spiritual realities within which we live between falling asleep and waking up. . . .

Between the change of teeth and puberty something forms itself on the soul level which can in a certain way be grasped through imagination. One receives experiences through imagination about what forms itself there in the human soul. The experience which I just described referring to the state between falling asleep and waking up is only one of the experiences which one has through imaginative cognition. In those interesting states that take place in the child from the change of teeth until puberty, there we see how a strong battle is going on in the process of becoming a human being. In this period of life, the ether body, which runs through her special organization until puberty, fights, so to say, against the astral body. It is a real state of battle which takes place in the child. And if we envision what corresponds to this state of battle on the physical level, we can say at this period of life there is a great battle taking place in the child between the forces of growth and those forces that play into us through physical inspiration, through the breath. This is a very significant process in the human inner core, a process which will have to be studied more and more if we want to know the human being. For what in part becomes free on the soul level through the change of teeth are the forces of growth. Of course, a considerable portion of these forces of growth still remain in the physical body and manage growth there. One part becomes free at the change of teeth and appears as soul forces.

Whatever continues to function as forces of growth in the child opposes something which now appears in the child essentially through the breathing process. What appears there in the breathing process could not appear at a younger age. Certainly the breathing process also exists in the child. But as long as the child has the forces in her physical growing and bodily organizing which then emerge at the change of teeth, nothing takes the place of what later is caused by the breathing process in the human body in such a striking, significant way.

As I said, before the change of teeth, what the breathing wants to effect in us cannot become active in the human organism. But then a battle begins of the forces which remained growth forces against the penetration of what out of the breathing process penetrates into the human being. For the first great significant step that appears on the physical level as a consequence of the breathing process is sexual maturity.

Natural science has not yet understood this connection of breathing and puberty. However, it certainly exists. In a way, we breathe in what makes us sexually mature, but also what, in a larger sense, gives us the possibility of entering into a lovingly embracing relationship with the world. That is what we really breathe in. There is also something spiritual in each process of nature. So, in the breathing process there is something spiritual and something soul-spiritual. This soul-spiritual element enters into us through the breathing process. It can only enter into us when those forces have become soul forces which earlier were working on the physical organism and which at the change of teeth ceased to do that. It is then that what wants to come out of the breathing process streams into the human being.

However, this is being opposed—and that's where the battle comes in—by what comes out of the growth processes, those that have remained growth processes. In other words, that which wants to come out of the breathing process battles against what arises out of the ether forces. This battle takes place between the ether forces, those forces that arise out of our ether body and which correspond on the physical level to the material system, the metabolic system, and the blood circulation, and the astral forces. There the metabolism plays into the circulatory and the rhythmic systems. So that we can say schematically: We have our metabolic system which plays into our blood system, in the blood-rhythm system. . . This is what rushes up from the part of the ether body in the human being, so to say, at this time between age seven and fourteen.

The astral body resists this. We then have the rhythmic element that comes from the breath streaming in. This battle takes place between the blood circulation and the breathing rhythm. This is what takes place inwardly in the human being at this time of her life.

If one speaks a little bit in images, one can say in a perhaps seemingly radical image that it is approximately between the ages of nine and ten when what took place in skirmishes before the main battle will then become the main battle in each child. The main battle between the astral body and ether body occurs between the ages of nine and ten.

That is why this period, this moment in time, is so important for the teacher to observe. It is so that, as a teacher and educator, one has to be carefully aware of what takes place between the ages of nine and ten, because the interaction happens differently in almost every human being. In each child one sees something very special. Certain qualities of temperament reach a certain metamorphosis. Certain ideas arise. Earlier it was not good to let the child notice anything of the difference between the ego and the outer world. But above all, it is at this time when one should begin to point out this difference between the ego and the outer world. While before it was good to speak to the child in fairy tale images and so on, as one personified and explained the events of nature as if they were like human events, now one can begin to teach the child in a more didactic, direct way about nature.

Natural history, even in its most elementary form, should only be taught to the child beginning at this time. For when the child begins in the first period of her life to sense her ego distinctively, she is really only beginning to feel the ego. At this point in time it happens that the child connects a sharply contoured concept—of course, more or less sharply contoured concept—with this ego. It is only at this time that the child learns to distinguish herself clearly from the outer world. At the same time as this experience, a corresponding experience occurs, that of the breathing rhythm and the circulation rhythm, the astral body and the etheric body storming against each other.

These things always have two sides in the human being. One side shows itself in the state between waking up and falling asleep. I have just now described that state. In the state between falling asleep and waking up, things are somewhat different. The child moves toward *imagination* and then develops something of *inspiration*. When we discern what happens through *inspiration* through the breathing process which corresponds to it on the physical level, we find that really only at this time—which for one child comes a little earlier, for another a little later, but on the average between age nine and ten—we find that at this time a real separation of the ego and the astral body from the etheric body and physical body takes place in sleep. The child is very intimately connected especially with her ego, with her physical and etheric bodies, even in sleep. But from this time on, the ego begins to light up like an independent being, since the ego and the astral body do not participate in the functions of the ether body and physical body.

Then we can say: This battle, which I have described, gradually subsides, beginning at age twelve, and with puberty the astral body comes into being in its own right in the human constitution. That which separates itself from the human being, that which later on takes less care of the physical, that is the same as what carries the human being through the portal of death into the soul-spiritual world when she

21

dies . . . . What separates itself there—individual subjects are presented in a materialist way—is being organized in the Ahrimanic direction especially in an age where the human being receives only materialistic and intellectual concepts, where intellectualism and materialism are already brought into the school, and individual subjects are presented in a materialistic way. Because we are asleep even by day with regard to our will and also to our instincts, the instincts become caught by what separates itself there. We train ourselves to conquer this life of instincts by taking in especially the spiritual-scientific concepts.

— GA 206/ 8-7-21, Dornach

Judgment

At puberty the astral sheath is pushed back, and the astral body becomes free. Now the young person begins to form the power of judgment so that a sure judgment can arise. But something else is even more important. What the human being has brought with him from his former life reveals itself in a special way so that in this life between birth and death he wants to deal with it. The human being at this time is not yet suitably equipped to observe the outer world in an objective way. But the way in which he faces the world is of a beautiful, idealistic disposition. In this way he tries to express himself, and it comes to expression as idealism, as hopes for this life. This hopeful expectation and this idealism show themselves in their true being during the period from age fourteen, fifteen to age twenty-one, twenty-two. At this time everything that wants to come out in this way comes alive, even if it is in contradiction to the reality of current life. They are memories of former lives stimulated by the new, fresh forces of the astral body. Woe to the human being whose ideals of his dreams and his expectations at that time are thwarted, who is told that a large part of these hopes will later on be judged only as youthful illusions, that they have no real validity and are only dreams that cannot be fulfilled! That's not what matters, it does not matter whether the ideals can be fulfilled, but it is a question of the forces which lie in them. These are beneficial, stimulating life forces which, if they are well nurtured, make our astral body secure and firm for the rest of life. When we have these ideals, then this member of the human organization becomes strong. There is nothing worse than not to enable the idealism to unfold at this time, and to meet this idealism as a Philistine who will try to suppress this idealism.

— GA 304A/8-30-24, London

Performing Deeds Larger Than Our Thoughts

Let's first of all look at the difference between a human being who in a certain sense is full of idealism, who sets high ideals for himself, and a human being who in general has an aversion to setting high ideals for himself, who only acts out of outer motivation, so to say. Let's say he eats when he is hungry, he sleeps when he is sleepy, he does this or that whenever these or those passions or instincts urge him to do that . . . . The idealist always has something in his ideals that he thinks about, to which he attaches his feelings, something that is larger, wider than his deeds. What makes an idealist in the spiritual-scientific sense is the fact that his thoughts are larger, more all-encompassing than his deeds . . . One can say the opposite of the person who lives in the other direction from the one just characterized: that he does not think in as large a way as he acts. He who acts only out of instincts, passions, urges, and desires and so on does not have an idea which encompasses all that he does in a given moment, but he performs a deed, a task on the physical level, that encompasses objects and events which he does not think about. His intentions, his thoughts, thus, are less wide, are smaller than his deeds, on the physical level.

Now the clairvoyant tells you the following about these two types of human beings. Whenever we perform a deed, a task in life which is larger, more encompassing than our thoughts, then this task always throws a mirror image into our astral body. Once we have gone beyond the action, we cannot do anything in life without having an image of the action in our astral body. The image later on communicates itself to the ether body. The way the image communicates itself to the ether body remains perceptible for the Akashic record, so that a clairvoyant can see the mirror images of the actions performed by a human being in the course of his life. Thus, mirror images also remain in the astral body which then continue onto the ether body of those persons whose thoughts are larger than their actions, that is the actions one performed out of idealism.

That is now the big difference between the mirror images of deeds resulting from instincts, desires, passions, and so on and the mirror images performed out of idealism: all of the former mirror images have something in a certain way destructive for our whole life. The images of our astral body are such that they gradually work back onto the entire human being in a way that they, one could say, slowly consume this human being. And these mirror images essentially have to do with the slow way that the human being in his life consumes himself until death, that is in his being on the physical level, while the mirror images which arise out of what from our thoughts goes beyond our actions have something revitalizing. Especially for the ether body, they are stimulating, for they are what continuously brings new revitalizing forces into our entire human being.

So, according to the descriptions of the clairvoyant, we have forces in our being on the physical level that, in fact, are desolating and destructive, and we also continuously have revitalizing forces in us. Now as a rule one can very well observe the effects of these forces in life. For example, there are human beings who wander around in life who are crotchety, hypochondriacal, of a gloomy temperament, who cannot cope with their own soul life, and this soul life works back onto their physical organism. They have become fearful, and one can observe how their fear, when it lasts forever in life, undermines the health of their organism all the way into the physical. In short, there are human beings who in later life are melancholic, of a gloomy temperament, who have a hard time with themselves, and are in many ways unbalanced individuals. If we now would research the causes of such a behavior, we would find that such individuals had little opportunity, in earlier periods of their physical existence, to experience what one can call an idealistic transcendence of their deeds by their thoughts, an experience of their thoughts being larger than their deeds.

In normal life one does not usually observe such things, but the effects definitely present themselves. The effects are there, and many a person feels these effects very strongly, feels them as the mood of his entire life, as the mood of his entire soul, and also in his bodily constitution. Thus, one could deny the astral body; its consequences cannot be denied, for one does experience the consequences. If in life what has just been described is seen, then people should realize that it is not so stupid to speak of such things as the line of reasoning that, even though the observation of supersensible events is only possible for the clairvoyant, the manifestation of clairvoyantly observed facts can always be demonstrated in life.

In contrast to this we see how the deeds which are smaller than their corresponding ideas leave such impressions and show themselves in later life as courage for life, confidence in life, and as equanimity in life. That passes over into the inside of the physical organism, and one only recognizes the connections if one observes life over a long period of time, if one does not only look at short periods of life. That is the mistake of many scientific observations in which one determines the effects of this or that already after what has happened in the course of only five years, while the effects of many things very often show themselves only after decades. Now consider that one has to say that there are not only people who are of just an idealistic nature, who in their thoughts go beyond their experiences. For we have a great number of experiences, for example, which can be grasped in ideas only with the greatest difficulty. So eating and drinking are something which is done daily out of desire, out of instinct, and it truly takes a long time until he who goes through spiritual development, so to say, includes these things in his spiritual life. It is just the everyday things which are the hardest to include into the spiritual life, for we will have eating and drinking included only when we can observe why we, in order to serve the whole course of the world, must take in in a rhythmical way the physical substances and what relationship the physical substances have to the spiritual life; how the metabolism is not only something physical but through its rhythm also has something spiritual in it.

However, there is a way to spiritualize gradually these things required not only by an outer material necessity. For there is the possibility of seeing these things in such a way that we say to ourselves: We are eating this or that fruit, and through our spiritual knowledge we can form a mental image of how, let's say, an apple or some other fruit stands in relationship to the totality of the universe. But that takes a long time. Then we will make it a habit to let food not only be a material fact, but we will make it a habit to observe what part, for example, the spirit has in the ripening of the fruit in the rays of the sun. Thus, we spiritualize also the material everyday processes and gain the possibility of entering with our thoughts even there; here I can only allude to how even there thoughts and ideas can be brought in. However, that is a long journey, and there are few individuals in our time who can manage to think about food in a fully valid way.

So we must say that there are not only individuals who perform instinctive actions and those who perform idealistic deeds, but each human being's life is so divided that he performs one part of his deeds in a way that the thoughts cannot come up to the level of the deeds and another part where the thoughts and the ideals have a greater scope than the deeds. Therefore, we have other forces in us which give our astral and etheric bodies revitalizing forces, forces which always shine a new light in our astral and etheric bodies. It is these latter ones which truly remain in our ether body as revitalizing forces. When we leave our sheaths with the spiritual part of our being after death, we have—in the first days after death—the ether body still attached to us, and through it we have a review of our entire life. And the best thing that now remains with us like an inner forming element is the aforementioned revitalizing forces which originate from the fact that our ideas went beyond the measure of our deeds. The ether body continues to have an effect beyond death in a way that further revitalizes us for the following incarnation.

Therefore, we may say that what we inject into ourselves as revitalizing forces that remain in the ether body is a continuing force of youth. And even if we do not prolong our life through that, we must say, however, that we can form our life so that it retains its strength of youth for a longer time, because we do many deeds in such a way that our thoughts surpass the measure of our deeds. If the individual asks himself how he can gain such ideals which best transcend our deeds, we can say that it is possible when we concern ourselves with spiritual science which leads us into the supersensible worlds. If, for example, we hear out of spiritual science about the evolution of the human being in our earth system, then such messages shake up forces in our higher members, and it is through this activity that especially at the present time we receive the most concrete, the most secure idealism. Take the question, what above all else does spiritual science serve? We can say: It pours youthful fructifying forces into our astral body and etheric body.

— GA 124 / 2-28-11, Berlin

The Law of Authority

Let's suppose we would not consider that the word "authority" must be a sacred one for the time between the ages seven and fourteen. If, thus, between the ages seven and fourteen we ignore such an important law, then out of an incorrectly developed ether body a correctly developed astral body cannot arise. And let us assume that we have to do with an individual who brought from former lives special forces, good strong capacities, talents that require an astral body which can catch fire for high ideals. If he sees an unjust deed in his environment, he can become inflamed with righteous wrath long before he can judge it with independent clear thinking. This reaction depends on the astral body. It is just these qualities of a healthy astral body which really ought to be available to this person, for he would need to set in motion what lives in him as a result of his former incarnations. Let us assume that we have neglected the principles which must be observed so that the astral body can be born capable of devotion and enthusiasm at the age of fourteen or fifteen. Then it becomes impossible to develop these talents because the astral body does not let these talents emerge—although significant talents, great capacities were given from before. The astral body does not have the forces or the currents which the ego, going from incarnation to incarnation, must use in order to unfold its talents.

— GA 118/ 1-30-10

The Astral Body and Mathematics

Everything that we take up in a mathematical way, through forms of lines, forms of angles, vertical, horizontal, what we measure, everything that we take up in a mathematical way, we develop in fact out of our inner core. It lies at the foundation of our inner being. . . . Then one does not say any longer that mathematics is an "a priori" knowledge. "A priori" means that something has been existing all along. If, however, one learns to observe inwardly, then one will know from where one has this curious mathematics: the astral body went through the mathematics of the whole universe, and thus, it has contracted again. We simply let emerge out of our soul what we experienced in a former incarnation, what then went through the whole cosmos, what then reemerges in the elegance of the mathematical-geometrical lines.

— GA 202/ 12-14-20, Bern

The Astral Body as the Source of Faith

Faith—what is faith? Faith is a soul force which can never be taken away totally from the human soul. It lives in each human being. There has never been a people which did not have it. No religion neglects to talk about it. It is the longing for faith which permeates the world. The soul always wants something it can hold onto. If this longing for faith finds no satisfaction, then the tortured soul is in dire straits. When what the soul can believe in is taken away, as it happens through materialism, then the soul feels as the physical body feels without air to breathe. This is the case except that the process of suffocation in the body is brief, while the one of the soul lasts a long time . . . . Because the human being cannot believe, because she has nothing to which her feeling of faith can hold onto, that is why the human soul is not healthy, and this unhealthy soul makes the body sick. This is how nervousness in today's sense comes about and becomes worse and worse. It is in this way that the soul has an effect on the body, and the person who has become this way has an effect on her surroundings, which she pulls down and makes sick. That is how it is that humanity degenerates more and more, and, unfortunately, it will become worse and worse. It is materialistic science which gives the human beings "stones for bread." The soul has no nourishment, while the intellect is overstuffed with knowledge. And such a human being then wanders around and does not know what to do with herself. She does not know where to hold on, and just as one takes the air away from her breathing, so the human soul suffocates from the fact that it has no nourishment, no spiritual life food.

Therefore, Anthroposophy came into the world in order to provide humanity with nourishment . . . . When we now consider this in view of the evolution of the world and of humanity, we must remember that during the Old Moon phase of the earth, the astral body was added to the human being. What now is this astral body? It consists of forces that always have to grasp something, that always have to hold on somewhere. In their effect these forces are what we experience as faith. The astral body is the source of faith itself. Therefore, it must receive nourishment in order to develop, in order to live. The desire for nourishment is the longing for faith. If this force of faith cannot be satisfied, then gradually faith will be deprived of what it could hold onto; if it does not receive good spiritual food, then the astral body becomes sick and through it the physical human being. If, however, it receives satisfaction from the concepts, mental pictures, and feelings which anthroposophy draws from the truth, from the depths of world knowledge, then it receives its appropriate soul nourishment; then it has its satisfaction. It becomes strong, and healthy, and the human being herself becomes healthy.

— GA 127/ 6-14-11, Vienna

The Effects of Occult Development on the Sheaths of Human Beings

The astral body may be described as an egoist. The consequence of this is that the development which liberates the astral body must reckon with the fact that the interests of man must expand and become wider and wider. Indeed, if our astral body is to liberate itself from the other principles of human nature in the right manner, its interests must include the whole of earth and earth-humanity. In fact, the interests of humanity upon the earth must become our interests; our interests must cease to be connected in any way with what is merely personal; all that concerns mankind, not only in our own times, but all that has concerned mankind at any time in the whole of its earthly development, must arouse our deepest interests; we must reach the point of considering as an extension of what belongs to us not only what belongs to our family by blood, not only what is connected with us such as house and farm and land, but we must make everything connected with the development of the earth our own affair.

When all the affairs of the earth become our own, we may give way to the sense of selfhood in our astral body. It is, however, necessary that the interests of mankind on earth be our interests. Consider two legends from this point of view. . . . When they were given to humanity at a certain stage, they were given from the point of view that the human being should be raised from any individual interest to the universal interests of the earth. The legend of Paradise leads the pupil directly to the starting point of our earthly evolution, when man had not yet entered upon his first incarnation, but when he is just beginning it, a time when Lucifer approaches him and he still stands at the beginning of his whole development and can actually take all human interests into his own breast. The very deepest problem of education and training is contained in the story of Paradise, a story which uplifts one to the standpoint of all humanity and imprints in every human breast an interest which can also speak in each. When the pictures of the legend of Paradise, as we have tried to comprehend them, press into the human soul, they act in such a way that the astral body is penetrated through and through by them; and under the influence of this human being whose horizon is expanded over the whole earth, the astral body may also make its own interest all that now enters its sphere. It has now arrived at being able to consider the interests of the earth as its own. Try, my dear friends, to consider seriously and earnestly what a universal, educative force is contained in such a legend, and what a spiritual impulse lies there.

It is the same with the legend of the Grail. While the Paradise legend is given to the humanity of the earth, inasmuch as it directs this humanity to the origin, the starting-point of its earthly development, and it uplifts us to the horizon of the whole development of humanity, the legend of the Grail is given that it may sink into the innermost depths of the astral body, into its most vital interests, just because this astral body becomes an egotist, which, if left to itself, only considers the interests that are its very own.

As regards the interests of the astral body, we can really only err in two directions. One is the direction towards Amfortas and the other, towards Parsifal, before Amfortas is fully redeemed. Between these two lies the true development of man, insofar as his astral body is concerned. This astral body strives to develop the forces of egotism within itself. But if it brings personal interests into this egotism, it becomes corroded, and while it ought to extend over the whole earth, it will shrivel up into the individual personality. This may not be. For if it occurs, then through the activity of the personality, which expresses its ego in the blood, the whole human personality is wounded and one errs on the Amfortas side. The fundamental error of Amfortas consists in his carrying that which still remains in him as personal desires and wishes into the sphere in which the astral body ought to have gained the right to be an egotist. The moment we take personal interests into the sphere where the astral body ought to separate itself from personal interest, it is harmful, and we become like the wounded Amfortas.

But the other error can also lead to harm and only fails to do so when the being who suffers this harm is filled with the innocence of Parsifal. Parsifal repeatedly sees the Holy Grail pass. To a certain extent he commits a wrong. Each time the Holy Grail is carried past, it is on his lips to ask for whom this food is really intended. But he does not ask. And at length the meal is over without his having asked. And so, after this meal he has to withdraw, without having the opportunity of making good what he had omitted to do. It is really just as though a man, not yet fully mature, were to become clairvoyant for a moment during the night, when he would be separated as if by an abyss from what is contained in the castle of his body and were then to glance for a moment into it; and as if then without having obtained the appropriate knowledge, that is, without having asked the question, everything were again to be closed to him. For then, even though he wakened, he would not be able to enter this castle again. What did Parsifal really neglect to do?

We have heard what the Holy Grail contains. It contains that by which the physical instrument of man on earth must be nourished: the extract, the pure mineral extract, which is obtained from all foods and which unites in the purest part of the human brain with the purest sense impressions. Now, to whom is this food to be handed? When we enter from the exoteric poetic story into the esoteric presentation of it in the Mysteries, it is really to be handed to the human being who has obtained the understanding of what makes man mature enough gradually to raise himself consciously to that which is this Holy Grail. Through what do we gain the faculty to raise ourselves consciously to that which is the Holy Grail?

In the story it is very clearly indicated for whom the Holy Grail is really intended. And when we go into the Mystery presentation of the legend of the Grail, we find in addition something very special. In the original legend of the Grail, the ruler of the castle is a Fisher King, a king ruling over fisher folk. There was another who also walked among fisher folk, but he did not wish to be the king of these fishermen, rather something else; he scorned to rule over them as a king, but he brought them something more than did the king who ruled over them—this one was Christ Jesus.

Thus, we are shown that the error of the Fisher King, who in the original legend is Amfortas, was a turning aside. He is not altogether worthy to receive health really through the Grail alone, because he wishes to rule his fisher folk by means of power. He does not allow the spirit alone to rule among this fisher folk.

At first Parsifal is not sufficiently awake to ask in a self-conscious way: What is the purpose of the Grail? What does it demand? In the case of the Fisher King it required him to kill his personal interest and cause it to expand to the interest in all humanity shown by Christ Jesus. In the case of Parsifal it was necessary for him to raise his interest above the mere innocent vision to the inner understanding of what in every man is the same, what comes to the whole of humanity, the gift of the Holy Grail. Thus, in a wonderful way between Parsifal and Amfortas floats the ideal of the Mystery of Golgotha. At an important part of the legend it is delicately indicated that, on the one hand, the Fisher King has taken too much personality into the sphere of the astral body, and, on the other, stands Parsifal, who has carried thither too little general interest in the world, and who is still too unsophisticated.

It is due to the immense educative value of the Grail legend that it could work into the souls of the students of the Holy Grail such that they had before them something like a balance: in the one scale was that which was in Amfortas, and in the other was that which was in Parsifal. They then knew that balance was to be established. If the astral body follows its own innate interests, it will uplift itself to that horizon of universal humanity which is gained when the statement becomes a truth: "Where two are gathered together in My name, there am I in the midst of them, no matter where in the development of the earth these two may be found." (*Matthew* 18, 20.)

— GA 145/ 3-26-13, The Hague

Puberty and the Brother-Sister Soul

I wanted to call your attention to forces at work in man's nature that we find at first in the regeneration of his organism as he sleeps. Now these forces are closely related to other forces that also develop in the human being with a certain unconsciousness. Those forces belong to human procreation, to the propagation of human beings. We know that up to a certain age a human being's consciousness is filled with a pure and straightforward unconsciousness of these forces—the innocence of childhood. Then at a certain age this consciousness awakens. From that time onward the human organism is permeated by an awareness of the forces afterward known as sensual, sexual love.

These forces that in earlier life live as sleeping forces only waken with puberty. These are the very same as those forces that in sleep regenerate the worn out or destroyed forces in the human being. Only they are hidden by the other parts of human nature in which they are mingled. These forces which are invisible in the human being can become capable of either good or evil only when they awaken, but they sleep, or at most dream, until puberty begins.

The forces that manifest themselves afterward must first be prepared with the rest of the forces of human nature; even though they are already intermingled from the time of birth, they are not yet awake. All this time the child's nature is permeated by these sleeping forces. This is what meets us in the child as such a wonderful mystery. It is the sleeping generative forces that only waken later on. One who is sensitive to these things feels something like a gentle breath of God in the activity of these forces—whatever the naughtiness, obstinacy, and other more or less unpleasant characteristics a child may have—working as if hidden in childhood and awaking in puberty. These innocent qualities of the child are those of the grown-up person, but in childlike form. One who recognizes them as among the generative forces feels the breath of divine powers. As long as these forces work in unconscious innocence, they are so wonderful, because they really breathe the pure breath of God, but in later life they appear in the human being's lower nature. We must feel these things and be sensitive to them, then we shall perceive how wonderfully human nature is composed. The generative forces, sleeping during the most tender age of childhood, waken around the time of puberty, and from then on are still active in innocence when the human being sinks back into sleep at night.

Thus, human nature represents itself in two parts. In each person we really have two people in front of us: the person who we are between waking up and falling asleep, and the other person who we are between falling asleep and waking up. In our waking state we are continually at pains to wear and worry our nature down to the animal level with all that is not pure knowledge, not pure spiritual activity.

What raises us above this part of the human condition lives as a pure, sublime force within the generative powers as they were during innocent childhood, and then in sleep these powers are awakened to regenerate that which has been destroyed by being awake during the day. So we have one part of us which is related to the creative forces in the human being and one part which destroys these forces.

However, the significant thing in the double nature of the human being is that behind all that the senses perceive we have to assume another human being, one in whom the creative forces dwell. This second part in which the human creative forces are living never really exists in an unmixed state, neither during wakfulness nor during sleep. For during sleep the physical and etheric bodies still remain permeated by the after-effects of waking life, by the disturbing and destructive forces. When at last the destructive forces have been removed altogether, we wake up again.

So it has been since what we call the Lemurian Age, the beginning, strictly speaking, when present humanity began its development. At that time, as is described in greater detail in *Occult Science*, the Luciferic influences on the human being began; from this influence there came, among other things, what today continually forces the human being to wear and tear himself down to the animal nature. The other element that exists in human nature, which man as he is now does not yet recognize—the creative forces in him— all this came into play in the early Lemurian time before the Luciferic impulses entered.

In looking at the present human being, we are rising to see the "becoming human being"; we go from the human being as a created being to the re-created human being.

In so doing we have to look out into that distant Lemurian time when the human being was as yet wholly permeated by the creating forces. At that time the human being came into existence as he is today. If we follow humanity beginning at that time of Lemuria, we have this double nature continually before us in all that has happened since. The human being then entered a kind of lower nature. However, at that time—this is shown to us by the clairvoyant view back into the Akashic record— a certain soul, like a brother- or sister-soul, was as if added to those human beings that were permeated by human creative forces. This sister-soul which had not entered human evolution was kept back, so to say, and not thrown into the current of human evolution. It remained permeated through and through by human creative forces only, and by nothing else.

Thus, a brother- or sister-soul remained behind. It could not enter the physical process of humanity's development. It lived on, invisible to the physical world of human beings. It was not born as human beings are born, in the flowing stream of this life, because if it had entered into birth and death, it would have been in the processes of physical human life. It lived in the invisible and could only be perceived by those who rose to the heights of clairvoyance, who developed those forces that awaken in the state we otherwise know as sleep. For then the human being is related to those forces that live and work in a pure form in the sister-soul.

The human being entered evolution, but above it lived a soul, sacrificing itself, which did not incarnate during the entire process of human life. It did not strive like ordinary human souls for birth and death in successive incarnations, and it could only show itself to them when they attained clairvoyant vision in their sleep. This soul had, however, an effect on human beings wherever they could meet it with special clairvoyant gifts. There were human beings who either by nature or special training in schools of initiation had this power and were able to recognize the creative forces. Wherever such schools are mentioned in history, we can always find evidence that they were aware of a soul accompanying humanity. In most instances it was only recognizable in those special conditions of clairvoyance where a human being's spiritual vision was expanded in sleep consciousness.

— GA 146/ 6-3-13

Earthly Maturity

Between the seventh and fourteenth years every human being passes through a process of growth and development which expresses, as strongly as in her case it is possible, the individuality she has brought down with her. That is why in this period of her life the child is thus somewhat closed to the outer world; and we teachers have the opportunity to observe during these years the wonderful unfolding of the forces of the individuality. But now, if this development were to continue after the fourteenth year, if the human being were to go on into later life with nothing further than this unfolding of individuality, she would become a person who was perpetually refusing and rejecting everything that approached her, a person utterly without interest in the world around her. That this does not happen is due to the fact that, during this period between seven and fourteen, she is all the time building her third body, which appears at puberty, and this third body is built up under the influence of the earthly environment. What appears as the relation of the sexes is not all of it. The exaggerated importance given to it is just a consequence of our materialistic turn of mind. In reality, all connections with the outer world which begin to make their appearance at puberty are fundamentally of the same nature. We should really speak, therefore, not of sexual but of earthly maturity. And under earthly maturity we have to include the maturity of the senses, the maturity of the breathing—and another such subdivision will also be sexual maturity. This gives the true picture of the situation. The human being, then, reaches earthly maturity. She begins to take again into herself what is outside and foreign to her; she acquires the faculty of being sensitive and not indifferent to her environment. Before this time, she is not impressionable for the other sex, but neither is she susceptible to her whole environment. It is then that the human being forms and develops her third body, her astral body, which is active in her until the beginning of the twenties.

— GA 317/ 6-25-24, Dornach

Change in Dentition

What is in fact this whole tooth formation in reality? It is a movement of the mineralization process from the inside to the outside. When the second teeth are all formed, then what pushes this mineralization process to the outside has come to its end. Then the sexual maturation process comes toward it which pushes inward. These are two opposing processes which work against each other in rhythm, the process of tooth formation and the process of sexual maturation. As the process of tooth formation ends, the process of sexual maturation happens in the other direction.

— GA 312/ 4-9-20

The Freeing of the Astral Body

If one now considers what happens in the stage of puberty, then one will have to say: here we see in a certain sense the opposite process to the one which happens at the change of teeth; we see how the desire forces of the human being, the instinctive character of his will, grasps his organism in a manner in which it had not been grasped earlier. We can condense this whole broad complex of facts and say the following: the body in which the desire nature slumbers, the astral body of the human being, is freed at puberty. It is the astral body which now, if I may say so, implants itself into the physical organism, grasps it, penetrates it, and thus makes desire physical, and which finds its expression in sexual maturation.

— GA 76/ 4-7-21

Inner Independence

Actually it is only at this moment in time (age nine or ten) where the child learns to see itself as separate from its surroundings, through feeling and will, through judgment. It is only at puberty when the child learns to distinguish itself from its surroundings by complete inner independence.

But in the development between the ninth and tenth year of life, one can see the beginning of this separation from the surroundings as a nuance. And that is why it is so important to be aware of this moment in time because one still has to hold the child firmly until puberty. Yet one has to begin to treat the child differently.

— GA 304 / 11-24-21, Oslo

Mental Picturing and Will Forces

If we ask for the quality of those forces which from childhood on are more and more being led into the head from the rest of the organism, we must find them mainly in the will forces, as we characterize these forces on the soul level. The rest of the organism continuously provides the mental pictures of the head with will forces. We can say schematically: We receive the head as a result of our former incarnation as carrier of the mental pictures, but the will forces are being sent in by the rest of the organism. What I have told you here does not happen only on the soul level but also shows its effects on the physical level. As much as we are head beings, we are being born into this earthly world as mental picture beings. However, the image-forming forces, as we are being born into this earthly world, are still very strong. They ray out from the head onto the whole of the rest of the organism. And it is these image-forming forces which have the effect in the first seven years of life, those same forces which consolidate the life of mental images in us, which are not yet consolidated before we have the second teeth. It is those same forces which lead us to the forming of the teeth. So that when the teeth come in, these forces become free. Then they can form mental pictures, and they can form the memory accordingly; then sharply contoured mental pictures can be formed. As long as we need those forces to form our teeth, they cannot become the forces that consolidate the life of the mental pictures.

Now we will have to see how—when we grow beyond seven or eight—the will, which essentially is connected to the other parts of the human being, would shoot into the head. This would not just simply happen. For our head, which is organized according to the non-earthly, would not be able to take up these strong forces which want to shoot into the head from the metabolism, which is the carrier of the will. These forces have to become dammed up first. These forces first must come to a stop before they are sufficiently thinned and ensouled, in order to be received by the head. At approximately fourteen years of age, the forces of the will become dammed up in the larynx; they show up in the human being in such a way that in the male body they show themselves in the change of voice. In the female they predominantly show themselves in another way. These are the will forces which come to a halt before they shoot into the head, so that we say: At the end of the second seven-year cycle the will forces get dammed up in our speech organization. Then they are sufficiently filtered, sufficiently ensouled, to become effective in our head organization. Then when we have gone through puberty and the voice change that goes along with it, we are so far that, through our head, mental picturing and will can work together in our earthly being.

You see how one gradually arrives at truly studying the interrelationships of the soul-spiritual and physical material, and how something like the speech-forming process can only really be understood when one recognizes it as the result of these two sources which feed the human being, those sources which, on the one hand, are in the head system and those forces, on the other hand, which are in the limb system.
— GA 201 / 5-1-20, Dornach

The Astral Body

At puberty what we call the astral body is being implanted into the physical body so that it takes hold of the body and causes those changes that constitute puberty.

What the human being goes through happens in the most manifold metamorphoses. Whoever has once truly understood such a process as the one that is expressed through puberty, a process which effects a certain new relationship in the development of the human being toward the outer world, will also recognize it when it occurs in a certain metamorphosis. What occurs in puberty takes hold of the entire human body and helps the entire human being to form a relationship with his surroundings; this process has been gone through earlier, I should say, in another metamorphosis at the moment when language developed in the child.

Yet what occurs in puberty occurs in the child in the formation of speech in another metamorphosis. There what in puberty grasps the whole human being and pours itself into his relationship with the outer world occurs between the rhythmic and limb system and the head organization of the human being. The same forces that in puberty grasp the whole human being and give him direction in his relationship to the outer world assert themselves between the upper and lower beings. And as the lower human being learns to sense the upper human being, in the same way that in later life he learns to sense the outer world, he learns to speak. One can observe outwardly in the human being at a later age a process, which occurred earlier within the human organism in learning to speak, that occurs in the whole human being in puberty.

And if one has understood this, then the possibility arises of understanding how the playing together of the lower human being—the rhythmic being and the limb being—in its interaction shapes an inner experience that is also outwardly present in nature that surrounds us. This experience inwardly of what is outwardly present leads one to the fact that what lives outwardly, taciturnly in things as their own language, begins to sound as human language in the human inner core.

— 4-7-21

Battle Between the Outer Will Element and the Inner Intelligence Element

A second phase in human life is puberty which in the male gender appears especially through the voice change and in the female gender in physical changes that are distributed over the whole body, in both cases around age fourteen. What is really happening there? What is it that changes after puberty? It is the whole of the human life of will. The entire life of will changes, otherwise the feeling of love could not enter the life of will. . . . When we research spiritually-scientifically what is happening there, we find the following: We grow together with the outer world more and more, especially in the time between the change of teeth and puberty; we grasp more and more of this outer world, and our will becomes more and more focused. We learn to bring our will into conformity with the objects and events of the outer world. If one truly studies the whole of this complex, then one finds that at that time the human being makes the will element his own through his interaction with the outer world, not from within. It was a profound intuition when a poet said,

> A talent grows in stillness; the character grows in the current of the world.

The talent sprouts from inside out; the character, that is the will element, forms in the current of the world, in the exchange of the inner forces with the outer forces. But the human being must defend himself against what comes toward him from the outer world. His inner core must react. The inner core must build a dam against what comes from the outer world. This will-creating element, which comes toward the human being out of the interaction with the outer world, is being opposed by an inner force; in the male this creates a dam in the larynx, in the female in other organs, and this damming, this colliding of the outer will element with the inner will element, expresses itself in the transformation of the larynx or similar organs. There you see how the spiritual in the outer world works on the human being.

Now you bring this together with the views of spiritual science which you already know. We know that through conception or birth we descend out of the spiritual-soul world into the physical. On the other hand, we know that concerning our astral body and ego, each time we fall asleep we go into a spiritual world. The spiritual world, which gives us our soul, worked on forming us until age seven, and from then on it becomes our intelligence. And it is the will element which opposes this intelligence already from birth, however especially strongly beginning from puberty, because it is then that the exchange with the freed-up intelligence takes place. And this battle between the outer will element and the inner intelligence element, between the spiritual state which we sleep through, which we pass through between falling asleep and waking up, and the spiritual state which we went through before our birth and conception respectively, the battle between what we have brought with us and what we sleep through each night, expresses itself in the forming of our larynx, in the forming of what is in the organism in puberty. The physical works together with the spiritual. We pass through a spiritual world from falling asleep to waking; in this spiritual world the will which we receive is hidden; in our organism is hidden the intelligence which through birth we bring with us into physical existence. Thus, we can understand the human body when we experience it as outer revelation of what takes place out of the spiritual.

— GA 199/ 9-18-20, Berlin

Sexual Love

She who, between seven and fourteen, did not learn to have such trust in human beings that will adapt herself to them, she will, in her later life, lack something of an inner strength and will energy which she needs in order to be truly strong enough for life. . . . She who from age seven to fourteen or fifteen, did not develop the possibility of looking up to another human being as an authority will not be capable of, in the next period of her life beginning with puberty, developing the most important thing that exists in human life: the feeling of social love. For in puberty not only sexual love arises in the human being but also what is the free social devotion of one soul to another. This free devotion of one soul to another must develop itself out of something; out of devotion it must wind its way through the feeling of authority.

Human beings without love and antisocial human beings come about whenever, between ages seven and fourteen or fifteen, the feeling of authority is lacking in teaching and training.

For our time these are things of the greatest and most eminent importance. Sexual love is, so to speak, a particular aspect, an excerpt of general human love. It shows itself as the specific which is connected more to the physical and etheric bodies, while general human love is connected more to the astral body and ego. But also the capacity for social love awakens without which there are no social institutions in the world.

— GA 192/ 6-15-19, Stuttgart

Cultivating an Inner View of the Human Being

One can study the turning point of life, puberty, when one finds how the process which comes to peak in puberty takes place in the organs. One can ask the following questions. What is shaping itself on the soul-spiritual level? What is created through the fact that the forces after puberty are no longer used for the building up of something in the organs, because the organs have come to a certain completion? What becomes of these forces which, so to say, were embedded in the organism until then? When one asks these questions, we can answer that these forces will become what lives in the special nature of the will impulses which will exist in a very different way after puberty than before.

Before puberty they are embedded in a very specific way into the organic processes. Afterwards they are no longer embedded in the organic processes, but they do not become free but rather connect themselves more intimately with the organism so that especially at this turning point in his life the human being becomes more the master of his organism than he was earlier. The will inserts itself into the organism in a more intimate and intensive manner than was the case before.

If one thus understands how the soul-spiritual interacts with the organic-physical, then one can study certain processes which are nothing else but the outer expression of what one perceives inwardly in the human organism. At the same time, one contemplates in such a way as to consider that concepts such as these, which are flexible within themselves, are also suited to become ever richer within, so that what is real can always be perceived. For example, we have here the process of the voice change which in the male individual is connected to puberty. There is a similar process in the female individuality, however spread out more over the entire organism. One only reaches a full understanding of these two processes if one sees in such a way how what happens in this change, through the voice change or in the female organism in other processes, is confirmed by the fact that the energy of will connects itself more inwardly and more penetratingly with the organism.

And at the same time one arrives at the understanding that what develops up to the change of teeth in its culmination expresses itself especially intensively in the formation of the human head, in which the development of the teeth is taking place, while what appears at the time of puberty takes hold of the whole of the rest of the organism with the exception of the head. When one sees it that way, it all becomes immediately clear. And through it one achieves an inner recognition, an inner view of the human being.

— 1-14-21

Changes in Muscle

And when age fourteen approaches, only then the soul-spiritual takes hold of the entire human being, and it is interesting to observe how beforehand the muscles adapted themselves to the heartbeat, pulse-beat, and breath. So then they begin, via the sinews, to make friends with the bones, with the skeleton, and adapt themselves to the outer movements. Just learn to thoroughly observe how a young person changes from his victory at the moment of death.

— GA 210/ 1-19-22, Mannheim

Several excerpts in this section taken from *Das dritten Jahrsiebt– Ausführungen Rudolf Steiners in seinem pädagogischen Vorträgen* (The Third Seven Year Period), The Bund der Freien Waldorfschulen, Stuttgart 1977.

The Liberation of the Astral Body

When the child enters the third seven-year period of life, the age of puberty, the astral body is liberated; on it depends the power of judgment and criticism and the capacity for entering into direct relationships with other human beings. A young person's feelings towards the world in general develop in company with his feelings towards other people, and now he is at last mature enough for real understanding. As the astral body is liberated, so is the personality, and so personal judgment has to be developed. Nowadays young people are expected to offer criticism much too early. Seventeen-year-old critics can be found in abundance, and many of the people who write and pass judgments are quite immature. You have to be twenty-two or twenty-four before you can offer a sound judgment of your own; before then it is quite impossible. From the fourteenth to the twenty-fourth year, when everything around him can teach a person something, is the best time for learning from the world. That is the way to grow up into full maturity.

These are the great basic principles of education; countless details can be deduced from them. The Theosophical Society will publish a book for teachers and mothers which will show how from birth to the seventh year the essential thing is example; from the seventh to the fourteenth year, authority; from the fourteenth to the twenty-first year, the training of independent judgment.

At the Gates of Spiritual Science.
London: Rudolf Steiner Press, 1906

Development of Judgment

With the age of puberty the astral body is first born. Henceforth, the astral body in its development is open to the outside world. Only now, therefore, can we approach the child from without with all that opens up the world of abstract ideas, the faculty of judgment, and independent thought. It has already been pointed out, how up to this time these faculties of soul should be developing—free from outer influence—within the environment provided by the education proper to the earlier years, even as the eyes and ears develop, free from outer influence, within the organism of the mother. With puberty the time has arrived when the human being is ripe for the formation of his own judgments about the things he has already learned. Nothing more harmful can be done to a child than to awaken too early his independent judgment. Man is not in a position to judge until he has collected in his inner life material for judgment and comparison. If he forms his own conclusions before doing so, his conclusions will lack foundation. Educational mistakes of this kind are the cause of all narrow one-sidedness in life, all barren creeds that take their stand on a few scraps of knowledge and are ready on this basis to condemn ideas experienced and proved by man often through long ages.

In order to be ripe for thought, one must have learned to be full of respect for what others have thought. There is no healthy thought which has not been preceded by a healthy feeling for the truth, a feeling for the truth supported by faith in authorities accepted naturally. Were this principle observed in education, there would no longer be so many people, who, imagining too soon that they are ripe for judgment, spoil their own power to receive openly and without bias the all-round impressions of life. Every judgment that is not built on a sufficient foundation of gathered knowledge and experience of soul throws a stumbling block in the way of him who forms it. For having once pronounced a judgment concerning a matter, we are ever after influenced by this judgment. We no longer receive a new experience as we should have done had we not already formed a judgment connected with it. The thought must take living hold in the child's mind that he has first to learn and then to judge. What the intellect has to say concerning any matter should only be said when all the other faculties of the soul have spoken. Before that time the intellect has only an intermediary part to play: its business is to grasp what takes place and is experienced in feeling, to receive it exactly as it is, not letting the unripe judgment come in at once and take possession. For this reason, up to the age of puberty the child should be spared all theories about things; the main consideration is that he should simply meet the experiences of life, receiving them into his soul. Certainly he can be told what different men have thought about this and that, but one must avoid his associating himself through a too early exercise of judgment with the one view or the other. Thus, the opinions of men he should also receive with the feeling power of the soul. He should be able, without jumping to a decision or taking sides with this or that person, to listen to all, saying to himself: "This man said this, and that man that." The cultivation of such a mind in a boy or girl certainly demands the exercise of great tact from teachers and educators; but tact is just what anthroposophical thought can give.

The Education of the Child in the Light of Anthroposophy. London: Rudolf Steiner Press, 1995.

Participation in Life

Today we must learn to let people participate in life; and if we organize education so that people are able to participate in life, at the same time setting to work on education economically, you will find that we are really able to help human beings to form a living culture. This, too, will enable anyone with an inclination towards handicraft to take advantage of the education for life that begins about the fourteenth year. A possibility must be created for those who early show a bent towards handicraft or craftsmanship to be able to participate in what leads to a conception of life. In the future, pupils who have not reached their twenty-first year should never be offered any knowledge that is the result of scientific research and comes from scientific specialization. In our days only what has been thoroughly worked out ought to have a place in instruction; then we can go to work in an out-and-out economical way. We must, however, have a clear concept of what is meant by economy in didactic and pedagogical matters. Above all, we should not be lazy if we want to work in a way that is economical from the pedagogical point of view. I have often drawn your attention to something personally experienced by me. A boy of ten who was rather undeveloped was once given over into my charge, and through pedagogical economy I was able to let him absorb in two years what he had lacked up to his eleventh year, when he was still incapable of anything at all. This was possible only by taking into account both his bodily and his soul natures in such a way that instruction could proceed in the most economical way conceivable. This was often done by my spending three hours myself in preparation, so as in a half hour or even in a quarter to give to the boy instruction that would otherwise have taken hours—this being necessary for his physical condition. If this is considered from the social point of view, people might say that I was obliged in this instance to give all the care to a single boy that might have been given to three others who would not have had to be treated in this way. But imagine if we had a social educational system that was reasonable; it would then be possible for a whole collection of such pupils to be dealt with, for it makes no difference in this case whether we have to deal with one or fourteen boys. I should not complain about the number of pupils in the school, but this lack of complaint is connected with the principle of economy in instruction. It must be realized, however, that up to his fourteenth year a pupil has no judgment; and if judgment is asked of him, this has a destructive effect on his brain. The modern calculating machine which gives judgment the place of memorizing and calculating is a gross educational error; it destroys the human brain, makes it decadent. Human judgment can be cultivated only from and after the fourteenth year when those things requiring judgment must be introduced into the curriculum. Then, all that is related, for example, to the grasping of reality through logic can begin. When in the future the carpenter or mechanic sits side-by-side in school or college with anyone studying to be a teacher, the result will certainly be a specialization but at the same time one education for all. But included in this one education will be everything necessary for life. If this were not included, matters would become socially worse than they are at present. All instruction must give knowledge that is necessary for life. During the ages from fifteen to twenty everything to do with agriculture, trade, industry, commerce will have to be learned. No one should go through these years without acquiring some idea of what takes place in farming, commerce and industry. These subjects will be given a place as branches of knowledge infinitely more necessary than much of the rubbish which constitutes the present curriculum during these years. Then, too, during these years all those subjects will be introduced which I would call world-affairs, historical and geographical subjects, everything concerned with nature-knowledge—but all this in relation to the human being, so that man will learn to know man from his knowledge of the world as a whole.

I most certainly do not long for the suppression of cerebral teachers; I am only calling attention to how cerebral teachers nowadays give their lectures with no regard to the fact that printing has been invented, and that what they give out in their lectures penetrates a student's brain-box better when read in a printed book. All the same, I point out that the best one can gain from a well-written book is hardly worth a tenth part of what comes from the immediate personality of the teacher in such a way that a connection arises between the soul of the teacher and the soul of the one who is taught. This can happen, however, only in a life of spirit with a basis of its own and its own administration, in which the individuality can fully develop and traditions do not hold sway for hundreds of years—as in universities and other centers of higher education—and where the individual man is able to be himself in the most individual sense. Then from this instruction by word of mouth will come something of which we can say: We have broken with everything coming to men, even through the arts of printing and illustration, but just by doing so we gain the possibility of developing quite new teaching capacities, which today are dormant in mankind. All this belongs, indeed preeminently belongs, to our present social questions. For only if we have the heart and mind for it shall we be able to enter into what is necessary for our present age.

Let us reflect how different our situation would be in life if what we have previously discussed here were to be carried out. Instead of our gaze being turned back to the most ancient epochs of culture, which took their shape from quite different communal conditions, from the age of fourteen or fifteen upwards, when the sentient soul with its delicate vibrations is coming to life, the human being must be led directly to all that touches us most vitally in the life of the time. He should have to learn what has to do with agriculture, what goes on in trade, and he should learn about the various business connections. All this ought to be absorbed by a human being. Imagine how differently he would then face life, what an independent being he would be, how he would refuse to have forced upon him what today is prized as the highest cultural achievement, but which is nothing but the most depressing phenomenon of decadence.

A Social Basis for Education.
Forest Row, England:
Steiner Schools Fellowship

Modern Education

After puberty, between the fourteenth and twenty-first years, not only the life of sexual love develops in man; this develops merely as a special manifestation of universal human love. This power of universal human love should be specially fostered when children leave the primary school and go to trade schools or other institutions. For the configuration of economic life, which is a demand of history, will never be warmed through as it should be by brotherly love—that is, universal human love—if this is not developed during the years between fourteen and twenty-one.

52

Brotherliness, fraternity, in economic life, as it has to be striven for in the future, can only arise in human souls if education after the fifteenth year works consciously toward universal human love, that is, if all concepts regarding the world and education itself are based on human love, love towards the outer world.

Upon this threefold educational basis must be erected what is to flourish for mankind's future. If we do not know that the physical body must become an imitator in the right way, we shall merely implant animal instincts in this body. If we are not aware that between the seventh and fourteenth years the ether body passes through a special development that must be based on authority, there will develop in man merely a universal, cultural drowsiness, and the force needed for the rights organism will not be present. If from the fifteenth year onward we do not infuse all education in a sensible way with the power of love that is bound to the astral body, men will never be able to develop their astral bodies into independent beings. These things intertwine. Therefore, I must say:

Proper imitation develops freedom;
Authority develops the rights life;
Brotherliness, love, develops the economic life.

But turned about it is also true. When love is not developed in the right way, freedom is lacking; and when imitation is not developed in the right way, animal instincts grow rampant.

You will find that most of our leading citizens were educated in the classical schools—Gymnasium (high school)—during the years when the soul is pliable and flexible. These classical schools were not born out of the culture of our age but of the Greco-Latin age. If those Greeks and Romans had done what we did, they would have established Egypto-Chaldean classical schools. They did not do that; they took the subjects for their teaching from immediate life. We take them from the previous period and educate people accordingly. This is very significant, but we haven't recognized it. Had we done so, a note would have sounded within the feminist movement that did not resound, and that is: Men, if their intelligence is to be specially trained, are sent into antiquated schools. There their brains become hardened. Women have the good fortune of not being admitted into the classical schools. We want to develop our intelligence in an original way. We want to show what can be developed in the present age if we are not made dull in our youth by Greco-Latin classical education.

These words did not resound, but in their place: Men have crept into and hidden under the Greco-Latin classical education, so let us women do the same. Let us also become students of the classical schools.

So little has understanding spread for what is necessary! We must realize that in our present time we are not educated for our age but for the Greco-Latin culture. This is inserted into our lives. We must sense it. We must sense what, as Greco-Latin culture, acts in the leading people of today, in the so-called intellectuals. This is one aspect of what we carry within us in our spiritual education. We read no newspaper that does not contain Greco-Latin education, because, although writing in our national idiom, we actually write in the Greco-Latin form.

Education as a Social Problem.
Hudson, N.Y.: Anthroposophic
Press, 1969.

The Heart of Childhood, Seven to Fourteen

The second period, from the change of teeth to adolescence, is spent with the unconscious assumption: the world is beautiful. And only with adolescence dawns the possibility of discovering: the world is true. Thus, it is not until then that education should begin to assume a "scientific" character. Before adolescence it is not good to give a purely systematizing or scientific character to education, for not until adolescence does man attain a right and inward concept of truth.

In this way you will come to see that as the child descends into this physical world out of higher worlds, the past descends with him, that when he has accomplished the change of teeth the present plays itself out in the boy or girl of school age, and that after fourteen the human being enters a time of life when impulses of the future assert themselves in his soul.

If this were not so, real education and teaching would be utterly impossible. For suppose we had to teach and educate the whole of the spirit which man brings into the world only in germ; then our stature as teachers would require us to be equal to whatever the human beings in our care might become. If this were so, you might as well give up teaching at once, for you could only educate people equal in brilliance and ability to yourselves. But you must, of course, be ready to educate people who, in some ways, are much more clever and brilliant than you are. This is only possible if in education we have to touch only one part of man, for we can educate this one part even if we are not as clever, as brilliant, perhaps not even as good, as the child potentially is. The thing we can accomplish best in our teaching is the education of the will and part of the education of the feeling life. For we can bring what we educate through the will—that is through the limbs—and through the heart, that is, through part of the chest of man—to the stage of perfection we have reached ourselves. And just as a man servant (or even an alarm clock) can be trained to awaken a much cleverer man than himself, so a person much inferior in cleverness, or even in goodness, can educate someone who has greater possibilities than he. We must of course realize that we do not need to be equal to the developing human being in intellectual capacity; but as, once again, it is a question of the development of the will, it is for the attainment of goodness that we must strive to the uttermost. Our pupil may become better than we are, but he will very probably not do so unless in addition to the education we give him he gets another education from the world or from other people.

Study of Man.
London: Rudolf Steiner Press, 1966,
now *Foundations of Human Experience*.
Anthroposophic Press, 1996.

Teaching Economically

The heretical statement, namely that it is rather obvious that you have to know the meaning of something that you are supposed to remember, is aimed particularly at teachers. But there is something else to consider: what is assimilated as meaning only works on the faculty of observation, the faculty of cognizing through thought; by laying emphasis on the meaning we educate a person one-sidedly merely to observe the world, to know it through thought. So if we were to teach only in accordance with that statement, the result would be nothing but weak-willed individuals. Therefore, the statement is right in a way and yet not entirely correct. To be absolutely correct we should have to say: If you want to do the best you can for an individual's faculty of cognizing through thought, you will have to analyze the meaning of everything that he is to take in and retain. It is indeed a fact that by first one-sidedly analyzing the meaning of everything, we can go a long way in the education of man's observation of the world. But we would get nowhere in educating his will, for we cannot force the will to emerge by throwing a strong light on the meaning of anything. The will wants to sleep; it does not want to be awakened fully by what I might call the perpetual unchaste laying bare of meaning. Thus, it is simply a necessity of life that penetrates beyond the simple truth about the revelation of meaning and gives rise to the fact that we must also do things with the children that do not call for the laying bare of meaning. Then we shall educate their will.

Unfortunately, we cannot straightaway found a university with all the usual faculties to follow on from the Waldorf school. So it will be up to us to prepare our pupils for other institutes of further education that they will have to attend when they leave the Waldorf school and before they step out into life. Thus, we must bring our pupils to the point when they leave of having the necessary qualifications for whatever further education institution will be suitable for them when they go out into life. We shall, nevertheless, achieve our aim and accomplish our task, despite the need to conform to these restrictions, if we can put into practice something of the educational principles we have founded on the present cultural epoch of mankind's development. We shall only be able to achieve this, though, particularly with regard to the older children who come to us and who will soon have to be sent out into other institutions of life, if we apply a golden rule: Teach economically.

We shall be able to teach economically if, particularly with the thirteen-, fourteen- and fifteen-year-olds we carefully eliminate everything that is merely ballast for human soul development at that age and can bear no fruits for life. For instance, we shall have to make room in our timetable at least for Latin, and possibly also for Greek. We must in any case really come to grips with language teaching, for this will be a most significant feature of our method as a whole. Let us look at the fact that you will be having pupils who will already have been taught French or Latin up to a certain stage. Their lessons will have been conducted in a certain way. You will now have to spend your first lesson or even your first week finding out what they can already do. You will have to repeat with them what they have done so far. But you must do this economically, so that each according to his capacity will benefit even from this repetition.

Now you will achieve a great deal simply by taking into account that what delays you more than anything else in foreign language teaching is translation from the foreign language into the mother tongue and vice versa. An enormous amount of time is wasted when, for instance, so much translation from Latin into German and from German back into Latin is expected of grammar school pupils. Instead, there should be much more reading, and the pupils should spend much more time expressing their own thoughts in the foreign language. How then will you set about teaching a foreign language, let us say French, on the basis of this rule?

Let us first consider the older children to whom this will apply, the thirteen- and fourteen-year-olds. For them you will first of all have to select carefully what you want to read with them in the language in question. You select passages for reading and then call up the pupils in turn to read them aloud. You will now save the pupils' time and energy if you do not at first insist on a translation into German of the passages in question, but instead see to it that each child reads properly with regard to pronunciation and so on. Next with the classes in which you want to let revision intermingle with new ground to be covered, it would be good if you still did not turn to translation but instead let the pupils give a free rendering of the content in the passage they have read. Just let the children repeat in their own words what the passage contains while you listen carefully in case anything is omitted that might indicate that something has not been understood. It is more convenient for you, of course, simply to let the children translate, for then you soon see where one of them cannot go on. It is less convenient to watch in case something is being omitted instead of just waiting until the child comes to a stop, but you can, nevertheless, find out by this means whether something has not been understood, if a phrase is not rendered in the mother tongue. There will, of course, be children who make a very capable rendering of the passage; this does not matter. And there will be others whose rendering is much freer in the use of their own words; this, too, does not matter. This is the way we should discuss the text with the children.

Next we tackle the opposite procedure. First we discuss some subject with the children in their mother tongue, some subject that they can follow through with us in their thoughts and feelings. Then we can try to let the children repeat freely (depending how far advanced they already are) in foreign language what we have been discussing with them. In this way we shall discover how well these children, who have come to us from all sorts of classes, know the foreign language.

Now you cannot teach a foreign language in school without really working at grammar, both ordinary grammar and also syntax. It is particularly necessary for children of over twelve to be made conscious of what lies in grammar. But here, too, you can proceed very economically. Now although this morning in our study of man I said that in ordinary life we form conclusions and then proceed to judgment and concept, you can, of course, not give the children this logical teaching, but it will underlie your teaching of grammar. You will do well to discuss matters of the world with the children in a way that, particularly with the help of the lessons in foreign languages, will enable grammar lessons to arise as a matter of course. It is purely a matter of structuring such a thing in the right way.

We have come to know the three stages of human development between birth and the twenty-first year. We must be quite clear that, particularly in the last of these stages, in addition to the conscious realm, the subconscious plays a large part, a part that is significant for the whole future of the human being. By looking at this matter from another point of view I should like to make clear to you why this is so.

Just think how many people today travel by electric train without having the faintest idea how an electric train is set in motion. Imagine even how many people see a steam engine rushing by without having any clue as to the workings of physics and mechanics that propel it. Consider what position such ignorance puts us in with regard to our relationship with our environment, that very environment we use for our convenience. We live in a world that has been brought about by human beings, that has been formed by human thoughts, that we use, and that we know nothing about. This fact, that we understand nothing about something that has been formed by man and is fundamentally the result of human thinking, is greatly significant for the whole mood of soul and spirit of mankind. Human beings literally have to turn a deaf ear in order not to perceive the effects that are resulting from this.

It is always very satisfying to notice how people (now I do not want to offend anyone with my turn of phrase) from the better classes enter a factory and feel thoroughly ill at ease. This happens because there shoots up from their subconscious the feeling that they use all the things that are manufactured in this factory without having the slightest relationship as human beings with what goes on there. They know nothing about it. When you notice the discomfiture of an inveterate cigarette smoker (to take a familiar example) as he enters the Waldorf-Astoria cigarette factory, knowing nothing about what goes on so that he can be kept supplied with his cigarettes, you can be pleased by the fact that at least he can still dimly perceive his ignorance about the environment born out of human thoughts, the environment in which he lives and of which he uses the products. We can be glad if people enter and leave an electric train with a slight feeling of unease because they have no idea how it works. This sensing of discomfiture is the beginning of an improvement in this realm. The very worst thing is to experience and live in a world made by human beings without bothering ourselves about this world.

We can work against these things only by starting during the last stage of the lower school, by really not letting the fifteen-, sixteen-year-olds leave school without at least some elementary ideas about the more important procedures taking place in life. We should teach them in a way that leaves them with a yearning to be curious and inquisitive at every opportunity about what is going on around them, so that they use this curiosity and thirst for knowledge to add to whatever they already know. Thus, towards the end of the lower school we should employ all the different subjects in a comprehensive sense towards a social education of our pupils, just as we use the separate subjects in geography to build an overall geographical structure in the way I described in my previous lecture. In other words, we must not neglect to use the concepts learned earlier of physics and natural history to introduce the children at least to the industrial processes closest to them. In their fifteenth or sixteenth years they should at least have gained some idea of what goes on in a soap factory or a spinning mill. Naturally we shall have to proceed as economically as possible. It is always possible to condense out of the overall complicated processes a simple, generalized picture. I think Herr Molt will agree that one could teach children in an economical way about the whole process of cigarette manufacture from beginning to end in a few simple sentences that would then only need a little elucidation derived from the remainder of the subjects we have taught them. It is utterly beneficial for children in their thirteenth, fourteenth, fifteenth, sixteenth years to be given such condensed descriptions of different branches of industry. It would be very good if during these years they were to keep an exercise book in which to record the processes of soap manufacture, cigarette manufacture, spinning, weaving, and so on. They need not be taught about mechanical and chemical technology on a grand scale, but they would gain a great deal from keeping such an exercise book. Even if the book were later to be lost, a residue would remain. They would not only have the benefit of knowing these things, but, more important, they would feel as they went through life and their profession that they had once known these things, that they had once been through the process of learning about them. This affects the assurance with which a person acts; it affects the self-possession with which he takes his place in the world. It is very important for his willpower and his capacity for making decisions. No profession is without people of efficiency and initiative who occupy their place in the world with a feeling about things which they do not actually need for their own profession but which they once knew about, even if only in a primitive way. Even if they have forgotten it, something will still remain. However, we do learn a lot in school. And in object lessons, which so often degenerate into platitudes, such things are also taught to pupils. But in these cases it can be found that later no feeling remains that says: I once learned about that and how fortunate I was to have done so. Instead the feeling is: Thank God I have forgotten all that; what a good thing that I have forgotten what I learned then. We ought never to be responsible for arousing this feeling in a person. If in our childhood we were taught in a manner that took account of what I have just said, then when we later enter a factory or something similar, innumerable things will shoot up out of our subconscious. Today everything is specialized in life. This specialization is actually dreadful. And the main reason why so much in life is specialized is because we start to specialize already in the way we teach in schools.

The gist of these remarks might well be summarized in the words: Every single thing a child learns during the course of his schooling should in the end be presented so broadly that threads may everywhere be found linking it with practical human life. Very many things that are now unsocial in the world would be made social if we could at least touch upon an insight into matters that later need not have any direct bearing on our own work in life.

No child should pass beyond his fifteenth year without having gone through the stage of writing specimen examples of practical business letters. Do not say that the children can learn to do this later. Yes, by overcoming dreadful obstacles they can learn it later, but only if they can overcome these obstacles. It is of great benefit to the children if you teach them to let their knowledge of grammar and language flow into business compositions, business letters. There should be nobody today who has not once upon a time learned to write a decent business letter. He may not need to apply this in later life at all, but there really should be nobody who has not once been encouraged to write a decent business letter. If you satiate the children mainly with sentimental idealism between the ages of thirteen and fifteen, they will later develop an aversion to idealism and become materialistic people. If you lead them during these years into the practical things of life, they will retain a healthy relationship to the idealistic needs of the soul, since these can only be wiped out if they are senselessly indulged in during early youth.

So, relatively healthy instincts regarding food still live in children during the early years of school. For the sake of the individual's development these instincts fade away during the thirteenth, fourteenth, fifteenth years. And when puberty finally overtakes the child this also means that he has lost his good instincts with regard to food, that he has to replace with reason what his instincts gave him during earlier years. This is why you can, as it were, intercept the last manifestations of the growing child's instincts for food and health during his thirteenth, fourteenth, fifteenth years. You can still just catch the tail end of his healthy instincts for food, for growth, and so on. Later you can no longer reach an inner feeling for proper nutrition and health care. Therefore, during these years the children must receive in school some instruction on nutrition and health care for the human being.

Practical Advice to Teachers.
London: Rudolf Steiner Press, 1976.

Developing Universal Love

Again at the time of puberty, one must be able to experience the birth of something even higher in human nature, of something which has been working up until then on the further transformation of the human organism. Whether one calls what comes to birth in the fourteenth to fifteenth year the astral body, and whether one likes such a name or finds it in bad taste, is of no significance. What does matter is that one becomes conscious of the fact that just as around the seventh year the intellectual element is born through the etheric body, now, around the fourteenth to fifteenth year, the entire body-free soul-being of man is born. Before that time feeling and willing were closely bound up with the physical organism. Just as up to the seventh year thinking was closely linked to the physical organism, so, up to puberty, feeling and willing are closely connected with the physical organism. Before the onset of puberty, that is "before school-leaving age," we must be careful not to allow certain elements to enter the pupils' thinking, which is then emerging step by step together with the emerging etheric body, elements which, in a certain sense, stem from a premature independence of feeling and willing. If the child is educated with loving care, supported by his sense of authority, and if he learns to develop his feeling and willing in dependence on the adult guide, his educator and teacher, then his own independent feeling and willing will be born at the right moment, namely at puberty. Children can rightly develop their feeling and willing only under the guidance of authority. If they are allowed to develop their own independent will prematurely, especially if what one could call certain secretive functions of the will intervene too early, damage for the rest of their lives will ensue. And if they are tempted to subject moral and religious impulses to their own judgments too early, they will make a premature contact with the finer organizations of their will.

I have to reaffirm that, up to the time of puberty, the child should learn to develop his moral and religious attitude under the moral and religious guidance of his teacher's authority. Only at puberty does the soul and spiritual life of the adolescent become sufficiently freed from the physical body for us to begin to allow him to make his own judgments. But as this affirmation runs counter to present-day trends, one meets prejudiced opposition everywhere. When, in public lectures in Germany at the time when that country was under the influence of a would-be revolution that never took place, I spoke about the child's natural inclination towards authority, my remarks were always met by an underlying feeling that all authority should be abolished, even in the case of children, who should be left to educate themselves democratically. My answer had to be that this was not at all what children really wanted. If rightly understood, they feel the need for guidance; they have an unspoken longing to look up to an authority and their love of authority is a distinctive feature of their natural makeup.

When the child reaches sexual maturity, love of the other sex becomes an obvious consequence. This general experience of love then will find its individual expression in the love of a man for a woman. But what appears as a fully justified fact in such an individual form at the same time is also an individual expression of a universal human love, of a love for all mankind. This universal love, as also the love for the other sex, begins to develop at puberty. The love of one human being for another can begin to develop as an independent force during puberty only, for it needs to be free from all authority. Such love is true devotion. Up to the age of puberty love is the result of an inner need; it has to be something which the child demands egoistically. We must realize that, up to the age of fourteen, the child has an egoistic desire to love. This means that he needs to feel the support of an authority upon whom he can depend and to whom he can be devoted, because such devotion fills him with pleasure. His love is the outcome of a natural urge. Everything he loves, whether it be all mankind, nature, stars, supersensible beings, pagan gods or God Himself, all that lives in him as love is, fundamentally, the content of his astral body. This astral body is born as an independent member at puberty. Up until then it was engaged in building up the individual human nature in the same way in which the etheric body was at work on the individual human nature up to the seventh year, up to the change of teeth.

The Renewal of Education.
Steiner Schools Fellowship/Kolisko, 1981.

The Danger of Too Early Incarnation of the Ego

What happens further is that the ego is set free—whether we call it the ether body or intelligence does not matter. This ego, so to speak, descended at birth, and streams into the physical body gradually organizes itself through and through. This means that there takes place a mutual permeation of the eternal "I" and that which is being formed, the slowly liberating intelligence, or the ether body is in the process of being born.

And then, looking at the ensuing age, the time from the seventh to the fourteenth year up to the time of puberty, we can say from a certain point of view that an element of will, a musical element is being absorbed; yes, this process is best described from one aspect when we say: what lies in the outer world is really the musical element, and all that which is being absorbed as music, as sound, is vibrating through the astral body. Through this activity the astral body is emancipated from the connection which it had up to this time with the whole organism. From another point of view we can, therefore, say with regard to the child: in puberty the birth of the astral body takes place. But once again, it is the ego which then, as an eternal being, unites itself with that which is being liberated, so that from birth to puberty, up to the age of about fourteen or more, we are concerned with a progressive anchoring of the ego in the entire human organism. From the seventh year on the ego fastens itself only to the etheric body, while before then, when the human being is still an imitator, the ego anchors itself precisely through this imitative activity in the physical body, and then later, even after puberty, the ego penetrates the astral body. So what takes place is the continuous penetration of the human organism by the ego, which can be seen really and concretely as I have described it.

This sphere has an immense significance for the educator. For, as I have indicated in my article on the artistic element in education in the last copy of *Social Future*, all education and teaching should always be carried out in the light of this gradual incorporation of the ego into the human organism as I have just described it; this process of the ego's incorporation in the human organism should be guided through an artistic education. What does this mean?

It means, for example, that the ego must not enter the physical body, etheric body and astral body too deeply, but that, on the other hand, it must neither be kept too much outside. If it settles down too firmly in the human organism, if the ego unites with them too intensively, man becomes too much an exclusively corporeal being; he will then think only with his brain, will be entirely dependent on his organism, in short, he will become too earthly, and the ego will have been too strongly absorbed by the bodily organization. That we must avoid. Through our education we must try to avoid everything that would lead to the ego becoming too strongly absorbed by the bodily organization, becoming too dependent on it. You will understand the utter seriousness of this matter when I tell you that the cause of the criminality and brutality of some men lies in the fact that their egos were allowed to be absorbed too strongly during their years of growing up. The characteristics of degeneracy, found by anthropologists and known to you, which manifest fully only in later years, reveal themselves often as an ego which has been too strongly absorbed by the rest of the bodily organization. And if there is such a man born with the earlobe of a criminal, it is all the more important that we see to it that his ego will not sink too deeply into the rest of his organization. Through a true artistic treatment in education we can avoid that. Even in a man with degenerate physical characteristics when this ego sinks too deeply into his organism, we can thus save him from becoming a criminal.

We can, on the other hand, fall prey to making the opposite mistake. There is a difficulty here. As we may place too small or too large a weight on one side of the scales—if the weight is too small, the other side will not rise; if it is too large, it will rise too high and we have to set the balance right—so, we have to face a similar fact in the realities of life.

Living reality cannot be contained in rigid concepts, and in trying to rectify one error we may always fall into the opposite. With regard to a child it is, therefore, the intimate factors of life which are all important, so that we never bring out one side or another too strongly but rather develop a feeling for the fact that in education one has to create an artistic balance. Because if one does not see to it that the ego unites with the organism in a right way, then it can happen that it remains too much outside, and the consequence will be that the person becomes a dreamer or follows fancies, or becomes altogether useless in life because he only lives in fantasies. This would be the other mistake, that one does not let the ego sink deeply enough into the organism. Even those who in their childhood showed a tendency to fancifulness, to false romanticism, can be protected from this by their teacher when he or she sees to it that the ego does not stay outside the rest of the organism, but penetrates it in the right way.

When one notices the well-known Theophosist's mark, which all children who are inclined to theosophy bring with them at birth—a small bump rising a little way behind the forehead—then one must strive to prevent this tendency to fancifulness and false romanticism through pressing the ego more strongly into the organism. But how do we bring about the one thing and how the other?

Balance in Teaching.
Spring Valley, N.Y: Mercury Press, 1982.

A Right Approach to the World of Ideals

Our deliberations so far will have made it clear to you that you must bring to your work an exact and detailed knowledge of man, a knowledge that includes also his physical and bodily nature. It may perhaps seem that some of the matters we speak of are a little remote from your everyday problems. This has to do with the fact that we are at this moment facing, as you know, a new and important task, the addition, namely, of a tenth class to the nine that we have already and that correspond to the "Volksschule." The new class will be composed of boys and girls of an age that requires very careful handling, and it is my earnest wish that these lectures should encourage you to enter upon a thorough study of this age of life, connected as it is with important conditions of development. You may think that this is surely a theme that concerns only those teachers who will be working with the new class, but that is a mistake. Our college of teachers needs to become more and more of a united organic whole. Every one of us must take his share in the whole education throughout the school, directly and indirectly. For if we simply continue, reasoning only from a different point of view, to arrive at the very same opinions and conclusions that were instilled into us by the events at the end of the 19th and beginning of the 20th centuries, then it will be impossible for us to take our part in the work that has now to be done to bring mankind out of its present misery. And if there is anyone to whom this applies more than another, it is the teacher, and especially the teacher who undertakes to guide the children on their way into the age of maturity, in other words, as they pass on from the ninth to the tenth class. As we have seen, however, in order to give this guidance in the right way, we have also to work towards it throughout the school.

It is imperative, at this turning-point in the history of our school, that we learn to conceive of our work in a deeper way than heretofore, and what I am now about to say does not concern only the higher but all the classes. We need to gather up our whole pedagogy, our whole didactics, and feel how there runs right through it all one single purpose, one single aim—to place into this world of ours human beings. This is our task, and we must be conscious of the grave responsibility it lays upon us. Without this, our Waldorf school will prove to be nothing but empty words. We may say all sorts of beautiful things about it, but we shall be standing on a floor that is riddled with holes, and in time the holes will become so large that there is no floor left to walk upon. We must find the way to make the whole thing true, inwardly true. This we can only do when we ourselves have a deep understanding of our vocation as teachers.

And here we must ask ourselves: What are we, as present-day human beings? We are the result of all that took place in the life of our civilization during the last third of the 19th century; we have come into this present time bearing that with us. What then are we all, my dear friends? Some of us have studied philology, have studied history . . . as these subjects were taught in the schools round about the beginning of the century. Others of us have gone further with mathematics and science. One has perhaps grown into what he is now by studying some particular method of singing, or again of gymnastics. Another, whose teachers had a strong bias in that direction, has been brought up to be a "gentleman" (probably with a rather physical and external understanding of the word), while the education of still another has been directed more to the inner qualities of mind and spirit, although through purely intellectual development. And all this education that we have received has gone right into us; we humans of today are, to our very fingertips, the product of it.

We have, however, now the task to understand what has thus been "educated" into us. We must see it for what it is, we must make ourselves master of it. This will require a searching self-examination, not of ourselves as individuals, but of ourselves as men of our time. Without undergoing this, we shall not be able to grow out beyond what our time can give us. And we must grow out beyond what our time can give us. It will not do to be mere puppets of the age, reflecting always the direction given to thought and culture at the end of the 19th and beginning of the 20th centuries. It is of the utmost importance that we should submit ourselves, as people of our time, to this conscientious self-examination and come to a recognition of where we stand as human beings.

Yesterday we were considering the conscientious self-examination, not as an individual but as people of this present age, which a teacher needs to undertake before he can be ready to confront a class of children of fourteen or fifteen years old. (I made it clear at the same time that the event of puberty has to be taken into account not only at the age when it occurs, but throughout the whole period of school life.) And I went on to show why this intense self-examination is so imperative in our time, namely, because the whole tenor of the education we ourselves received in the age that has just passed was such as to leave us without any understanding at all for the youth of the present day. Let us try to get a clear picture of the situation in which we find ourselves today in this respect.

Consider first of all a human being in his twenties, say, from twenty-one to twenty-eight years old. This period of life we denote in spiritual science as the time when the birth of the "I" takes place, the time when man's ego comes to full recognition. We explained yesterday how different for the boy and for the girl is the situation in regard to the ego round about the time of puberty. In the case of the girl, the ego is, as it were, dissolved in the astral body and not yet independent. With the boy, on the other hand, the ego lives a life that is withdrawn into itself. And the behavior that can be observed in girls and boys of this age is nothing else than the result of these inner facts. But when the ego, at about the age of twenty-one, begins to assert its importance, a new situation arises. At this age of life humans seeks humans; people seek, and find, their fellow human beings.

We understand this when we know that if a man or woman, let us say of twenty-four years old—or it may be a little younger, but not less than twenty-one—meets another who is also not more than twenty-eight, then they stand over against one another in similar reciprocal relationship, whether we are considering them from the point of view of body, soul or spirit. In this age of life, human beings meet as equals. Teachers should take pains to observe this fact wherever life gives them the opportunity. The absurd psychological nonsense that is so much studied by teachers today is just a piling-up of word-wisdom. If you want to understand life, you must study such phenomena as the one I have just described. See whether you cannot detect a delicate nuance of feeling in the mutual relationships of human beings between the ages of twenty-one and twenty-eight.

And now let us see how the matter stands when a boy or girl between the ages of fourteen and twenty-one meets a man or woman between twenty-eight and thirty-five. Here a relationship of complete equality is impossible. Nevertheless, under certain conditions (of which I will say more presently), a good and significant understanding can be established between these two age-groups. For the situation here is as follows.

The development that is taking place in the younger person under the influence of the astral body is, at this age, mainly unconscious. It expresses itself in outward behavior, in the whole manner in which such young people (who are but children still!) make their way into life. They become perhaps more and more skilled, or they begin to have great ideals. All this development and growing contact with the outer world goes on, as it were, under the spell of unconsciousness, just as the external growth and development of the body is unconscious. But now in the older person the same kind of development is taking place, only with him, it is inward, in the soul. And this is why a person of twenty-eight to thirty-five is best fitted to feel and perceive with his soul what is going on in a young person of fourteen to twenty-one. He is predestined for it. And boys and girls in their teens are on their part ready to look up to men and women of twenty-eight to thirty-five. For in these men and women they can see at work, inwardly, the very same kind of development that is taking place in themselves externally, in the physical body, and more unconsciously.

Among the Greeks this relationship was still a very common experience. Quite simply and instinctively, the boys and girls of fourteen to twenty-one looked up to the men and women of twenty-eight to thirty-five, feeling that these had in their souls what they themselves had in their physical bodies. Without being fully conscious of it, they recognized in the older person, in a more refined and intimate form, what was for themselves an outward experience. And the men and women who had reached the twenty-eight to thirty-five period, felt strongly drawn on their part to boys and girls in their teens with all the development they could see taking place in them.

Nowadays, human relationships tend to be abstract. Among the Greeks social life was much more instinctive. One person meant something to another just through the fact that he was older or younger, and relationships of this kind between different age-groups were a powerful factor in Greek life.

Let us try to picture for a little how life went on in this land of Greece. The child who was beginning to grow up into manhood would feel a reverence for a thirty-year-old. But as soon as he had passed his twentieth year, he would begin to feel a strong impulse to unite, instead, with those of his own age. This gave diversity to life. It gave also intimacy and inwardness. And it helped to build up the whole structure of society. That is an important point for us today. For what is our situation, we who no longer feel these instinctive relationships with one another? We teachers have no understanding for the children in their teens. We cannot solve the riddle that faces us in these boys and girls; for we have not yet the thoughts and ideas that can reawaken in us consciously those feelings that we had long ago instinctively and have been obliged to lose in the natural course of evolution.

The only hope is to bring anthroposophical-spiritual knowledge into the domain also of pedagogy and didactics. Unless we can do this, we shall merely go on widening the gulf between ourselves and these older children, until at last it will be so wide that we shall be forced to rely entirely upon our word of command. It may even go so far that we reckon on being able to fall back on the police if we cannot keep order; we may have to count on the children knowing that the police are there in the background. The only way for us teachers to attain the intimate kind of relationship that we desire with our pupils is to open our hearts and souls to the truths of spiritual science, for these truths can verily call up again in us consciously what was once given to man long ago in his life of instinct.

Yesterday, I told the teachers who are to take the tenth class that they should be ready to give the children the rudiments of a knowledge of man. It must, of course, be a knowledge that places man once again into the whole great universe, gives him his place and part there, in body, soul and spirit. To do this worthily, as true educators, we shall have first of all to study the current textbooks on anatomy, for example, and physiology. It is, however, most important that we use these textbooks merely as books of information, to bring us up to date with the achievements in the various sciences during the past hundred years, achievements that have, as we know, been arrived at with complete disregard of the spirit. And then we have to illuminate these achievements of science at every point with what we can gain from anthroposophy.

You will have to take up a completely different attitude towards all this modern scientific literature from the attitude that is common among teachers today. You will, of course, be taunted with being "superior," but that you must bear with. You have to accept the fact that, for you, all this modern science and culture are nothing more than a groundwork of information. You are really in the same position in regard to it as a Greek would be if he were to come alive again on earth today. He would point perhaps to our chemistry and say: "The knowledge I have of earth—that it is dry and cold, that it has influence on the plants—that knowledge you elaborate on and particularize. It is, of course, quite interesting to develop this detailed, specialized knowledge of the earth element. But you know nothing of the working of the whole; your knowledge extends no further than over one fourth of the whole."

It is really high time we got back to this more living kind of knowledge, a knowledge that can find its way into our intuitive perception, into our feelings and into our will, a knowledge that is, for the soul and spirit, what blood is for the body. As possessors of such knowledge, we become different men and women, capable of being true teachers and educators, which no automaton who mechanically follows all manner of artificially invented methods can ever be. The vocation of a teacher is not for him.

It has even gone so far as this today, that people make experiments because they want to come to their own conclusions. They experiment with memory, to find out how it works; they experiment with the will; they experiment even with thinking, to see how thoughts work. Quite nice little games—and certainly some results do emerge from it all. We need not look with disapproval upon games, either in children or in laboratories; but the narrowing down of the field of vision that is implied in all this—against that we must most emphatically protest.

In these studies I have had to make it clear that our work as teachers depends upon our own self-development, depends upon our own ability to take our right place in the world. And we have seen how at the turning point in a child's life that occurs in the thirteenth, fourteenth or fifteenth year, our success as teachers, even more than ever before, depends on having prepared ourselves to meet the boys and girls rightly at this important moment in their lives.

I have also explained to you that, in addition to this self-preparation of the teacher, we must arrange our whole work in the lower classes in such a way that the children themselves receive a right preparation for the event of puberty.

Everything depends, as you know, on the relationship to the world that develops gradually during the years of childhood. At the time of puberty, the child's attitude to the world finds expression in an inclination for ideals. Boys as well as girls begin at this age to show a desire for more than the world of the senses can give them. They want to reach out to something beyond. Even the very awkwardness of boys—as well as the corresponding qualities we notice in girls—are signs of this "feeling after" some supersensible ideal, some higher aim in life. That life must be there for some purpose, that life must have a meaning, is a conviction that lies deep in human nature; we must reckon with it. And we must also be alive to the danger that this deep intuitive conviction can be led on wrong paths. You will frequently find with a boy of fourteen or fifteen years old who is beginning to be haunted by all kinds of hopes and desires that his early training and education have been such as to encourage in him the feeling that he knows quite well how things ought to be. The girl, too, begins to pass judgment upon life around her. Girls are, in fact, severe critics of life at this age. They think they know perfectly well what is right and what is not right, and more especially what is just and fair and what is unjust and unfair. They lay down their opinions about everything around them, and they are in no doubt whatever that life will give them the possibility of placing something new into the world, something that will have its source outside of everyday life, in the land of ideals. So strong at this age is the turning to ideals—and ideas.

A right approach to the world of ideals will, however, only be possible for our children if we have prepared them for it during their previous years of school. And for this purpose, we must be able to steep our own thought and feeling in those basic facts of human life that can give us insight into the growth and development of the child. Theoretically, we learn from spiritual science of three cardinal aspects of the child's development. We learn how, up to his seventh year, he is a being who imitates. He grows by doing what he sees done around him. Indeed, the whole activity of a little child is nothing but imitation. At the period of the change of teeth, he begins to feel a need to follow an authority. He wants to hear from those around him what he is to do. Whereas hitherto he has received into himself and imitated, as a matter of course, whatever went on around him, good or bad, true or false, now he begins to listen to what is spoken in his presence and obey that. At puberty, a further stage is reached. The child begins to feel that he can judge for himself. He still, however, needs to feel the support of authority behind him; but the authority must be chosen by himself, must commend itself to him as self-evident. He must be able to say: "That is a person I can rely on when it is a question of forming an opinion." Now it is for us to see that the young child grows up into the natural acceptance of authority in the right way.

When a child attains puberty, he should at the same time undergo a change through the fact that he is now about to dispense with authority; he has outgrown it. But if we have not in the earlier years accustomed him to the acceptance of authority, this important change will be missed. He must first experience the dependence on authority; then at puberty he can outgrow this feeling of dependence and begin to judge for himself.

And this will mean that the time has come for us teachers to enter into a new relationship with the children, a relationship that is well expressed in the familiar saying: "*Ein jeglicher sich seinen Helden wahlt, dem er die Wege zum Olymp sich nacharbeitet.*" (Each one of us chooses his own hero, in whose footsteps he will follow on the path to Olympus.) This change in relationship can obviously bring us often into troublesome situations with the children. We no longer have it in our power to be their ideal as a matter of course. We have to see that we live up to it! Hitherto we have been able simply to give orders. Now the children begin to take note of our behavior; they begin to have a very sensitive perception for faults or lapses on the part of the teacher. Yes, there is this danger, and we must face it quite consciously. Boys and girls of this age are particularly sensitive to the teacher's mood, to his attitude of mind. If, however, we are not bothering about ourselves in an egotistic way, but are intent on dealing honorably with the children, then we shall accept the situation and reckon always with the possibility of sensitiveness.

In that way we shall find we can establish a free relationship with the growing boy and girl.

Thus, we shall be able to bring about that our children grow in the right way into the true, which they bring with them as an inheritance from the spiritual world; they then unite themselves aright with the beautiful; and finally they learn also—here in this world of sense existence—the good. For it rests with them to impress the good upon the world into which they have come. It is a downright sin to speak in an abstract way of the true, the beautiful, and the good, without showing clearly and practically how these three are related to the different ages of childhood.

Supplementary Course.
Forest Row, England:
Steiner Schools Fellowship, 1956.

Sexual Maturity

Nowadays, in this age of rather materialistic thought, sexual maturity is a much discussed topic. The subject is generally treated in isolation, yet to unencumbered observation it is in fact nothing less than the complete metamorphosis of human life at that particular age. Adolescents do not only develop soul-spiritually or physically conditioned erotic sensation. They begin to form judgments directly from out of their personality at this stage, relating to the world through sympathy and antipathy. For the first time they are placed out in the world. They become able to give themselves to the world in such a way that independent thinking, feeling, and willing in relation to the world can now proceed them.

The time between changing their milk teeth and sexual maturity is one primarily based on an implicit feeling for authority towards the teacher, the educator. This important age bridges, in a certain sense, two polar opposites. On the one hand we have childhood, during which the children are abandoned to objectivity, without in any way feeling themselves to be the subject. On the other hand, they approach maturity when, with varying degrees of clarity, they separate themselves and their entire inwardness from the outer world. This is achieved through all that can be brought under the heading of sympathy and antipathy—all the expressions and manifestations that we call love. Between these two stages, these two poles, lie the years of compulsory schooling, a time when we have to effect this transition through education, by means of the lessons.

At both these stages, in childhood and at physical maturity, each person has a certain point of gravitation in their lives. During childhood it lies outside with the world, at maturity within themselves. The time between these two points, that of compulsory schooling, is when individuals, complete with their soul life, are in a somewhat unstable state of balance, an equation in which the teacher only belongs. When teachers can teach from out of a background of true knowledge about human beings, they will successfully make the transition for the child to reach maturity with the inbuilt urge to become a practical human being.

This is why we try to introduce practical work throughout Waldorf schools in the years leading up to puberty. We bring in crafts and handwork that are approached from an artistic angle. I would like to say at this point that if one follows the phenomenon of blushing and going pale as it were inwards, one sees the result of all that the teacher, in his role of implicit authority, of didactic and pedagogical artist, has shaped within the child's soul and spirit between the change of teeth and sexual maturity. Morality is not taught. Morality is lived. Goodness is transferred into sympathy and antipathy from teacher to pupil. This lives on in the soul's internal blushing and growing pale, when the inner sense of life is jeopardized, destroyed or lamed by some threat, or by something of which one is ashamed. In this way a feeling, a complex of feelings, develops within the child in response to real, true human dignity. It is of the greatest importance, within the finely balanced relationship between children and their teacher, that living morality develop. For when the child reaches sexual maturity, what I yesterday characterized as an ether body in time, as a time organism, is faced with what is now a sort of higher member of the human composition. At physical maturity what is known in anthroposophy as the astral body, and what has placed the individual out into the world as I described, now approaches the ether body. All that has been shaped into a system of sympathy and antipathy by artistic means is now transformed into a moral attitude of soul.

You see, the wonderful mystery of sexual maturity is that the living moral we tended in the younger child becomes conscious morality, conscious moral principles at puberty. This constitutes metamorphosis on a grand scale. What happens in eroticism is merely a subsidiary expression of this. Only a materialistic age sees eroticism as the main issue. But the core issue must be found in that wondrous mystery, so that what we initially attributed to natural factors from direct experience can now emerge into the light of day as conscious morality.

Anthroposophically Based Education and Teaching Methods.
Forest Row, England: Steiner Schools Fellowship

Criticism and Compromise, Masculine and Feminine

It is all too easy to criticize life at the present time. Most people meet displeasing aspects of it every day, and one could easily feel tempted to make clever suggestions about how to put the world in order. But it simply won't do to educate pupils in such a way that, when they leave school to enter life, they can only criticize the senselessness of all they find there. However imperfect life may be when judged by abstract reasoning, one nevertheless must be able to play one's full part in it. Waldorf pupils, who have been treated as individuals perhaps more than is usually the case elsewhere, have to be sent out into life—otherwise there would be no sense in having a Waldorf school at all. But they must not become estranged from contemporary life to the extent that they can only criticize what they meet outside.

80

We have no intention of denying that in many ways the Waldorf school is built upon compromise, but as far as it is humanly possible, we shall always try to educate out of a true knowledge of man.

To continue, the morning sessions are arranged in the way already indicated. Because it is essential for our pupils to be able to move on to higher forms of education, we have to include in our curriculum certain other subjects, such as Greek and Latin, which are also taught in morning lessons. In these ancient languages "soul-economy" is of particular importance.

The afternoon lessons are given over to more physical activities, such as gym and eurythmy, and to artistic work which plays a very special part in a Waldorf school. I will give further details in the coming days.

We try, as far as this is possible, to teach the more intellectual subjects in the morning, and only when the children's headwork has been done are they given movement lessons, in as far as they have not let off steam already between morning lessons. However, after these movement lessons they are not taken back to the classroom in order to do more headwork. I have already indicated that this has a destructive effect upon life. For while the child is engaged in physical movement, supersensible forces are unconsciously working through it. And the head, having surrendered itself to physical movement, is no longer in a position to resume its headwork. It is, therefore, quite erroneous to believe that by sandwiching a gym lesson between other more intellectual lessons, one is providing a helpful change with its attendant benefits. The homogeneous character of both morning and afternoon sessions has shown itself to be beneficial to the general development of the pupils. If one constantly bears in mind the characteristic features of human nature, one will best serve human inclinations.

From what you have heard so far, you may have gained the impression that the art of education based on anthroposophical knowledge of man seeks to nurture above all a healthy and harmonious development of the child's physical body. You may have noticed that the following questions could be looked upon as guidelines for our educational aims: How can we assist the free unfolding of the formative forces, issuing from the head and working upon and shaping the young organism? How do we work in harmony with the child's developing breathing and blood circulation during the middle years? What must we do in order to cultivate in the widest sense possible the forces working throughout the child's muscular system? How can we rightly support the processes of the muscles growing onto the bones through the tendons, so that the young adolescent can place himself properly into the external world? All these questions imply that whatever we do to enhance the development of the child's soul and spirit is directed, first of all, towards the best possible healthy and normal development of its physical body. And this, indeed, is the case. We do aim in full consciousness to aid and foster the healthy development of the child's physical body, for in this way the child's soul and spiritual nature is given the best means of unfolding freely and out of its own resources. By damaging as little as possible the spiritual forces working through the child, we give it the best possibility of developing healthily. Not that we have our preconceived ideas of what a growing human being should be like. Whatever we do in our teaching is an attempt to create the most favorable conditions for the children's physical health. And because we have to pay attention also to the soul and spiritual element, because the physical must ultimately become its outer expression, its manifestation, we have to come to terms also with the soul and spiritual aspect in the way best suited for the healthy development of the child.

You may ask: From which educational ideal does such an attitude spring? It is the outcome of a total dedication towards human freedom. It springs from the ideal of placing the human being into the world in such a way that he can unfold his individual freedom or, at least, that no physical hindrances should prevent him from doing so.

What we are specially striving for in our education with its emphasis on the promotion of the physical development of the child is that our pupils should learn to make full use of their physical powers and skills in their later lives. Waldorf education rests upon the knowledge and the confidence that life in general will have the best chance of developing if it is allowed to develop freely and healthily. Naturally, all this has to be taken in a relative sense which, I hope, will be understood.

When the pupil leaves school at the age of fourteen plus, it is time for us to examine once more whether, during his school years from the change of teeth to the coming of puberty, we have done our utmost to help and equip him for later life. (During the coming days, when dealing with the aesthetic and moral aspects of education, we shall look more closely at the stage of puberty. Just now we will consider the more general human aspects.) We must realize that during his past school years we have been dealing mainly with his etheric body, with his body of formative forces, and that the soul life—of which more will be said a little later—was only beginning to manifest itself towards the approach of his school-leaving age. We must consider the next stage, which begins with the fourteenth to fifteenth year and which continues right up to the beginning of the twenties, a time in which the young man or woman has to face the task of fitting himself or herself more and more into external life. We have already seen how gradually the child takes hold of his body, finally incarnating right into his skeleton, and how, by doing so, he grows together more and more with the external world, how he learns to adapt to outer circumstances. Fundamentally, this process continues up to the early twenties, after which there follows a most important period of life. Although as teachers we now no longer have any direct influence over the young person, we have in fact already done a great deal in this direction during the previous years, and this will become apparent from the early to the late twenties.

After leaving school, the young person has to undergo a training for a particular vocation. Now he or she no longer receives what has mainly come out of human nature itself, but rather what has become part and parcel of the civilization we live in, at least with regard to a chosen trade or profession. Now the young person has to be adaptable to certain forms of specialization. In our Waldorf school we try to prepare this stepping out into life by introducing practical crafts, such as spinning and weaving, to our fourteen- and fifteen-year-olds. To gain practical experience in such crafts is not only important for a future spinner or weaver but for every person who wishes to be able to turn his hand to anything that a given situation may demand. However, it is important to introduce the right activities at the right time.

Now, what has been cultivated in a child's etheric body, or body of formative forces, during the early school years reemerges in the soul sphere of a young person during his or her twenties, that is, at the time when he or she has to enter a profession. The way in which he was treated at school will be largely instrumental in his responding to outer conditions—either clumsily, reluctantly, full of inhibitions, or skillfully and with an inner strength to overcome obstacles. During his twenties the young person will certainly become aware of how the experiences of his school years first went underground, as it were, while he was training for a trade or profession, only to surface again in the form of capacities, such as being able to handle certain situations or to fit oneself into life in the right way. A teacher who is aware of these facts will pay due attention to the critical moments in the life of the pupil between the change of teeth and puberty.

With the onset of puberty, an entirely new situation arises, with the effect that fundamentally the emerging adolescent is a totally different being from what he was before sexual maturity. In order to characterize the situation, it may be useful to refer to what was spoken of at the end of yesterday's lecture. Up to the change of teeth, it is normal for a child to live entirely within the physical body. However, if this state is extended beyond its normal time—and in later life such a situation would no longer represent normal conditions—the consequences will be a markedly melancholic temperament. During childhood it is natural to have the kind of relationship between the soul-spiritual and physical organization which is characteristic of an adult melancholic. We must always bear in mind that what is right and good for one stage of life becomes abnormal for another.

During the second dentition certain soul and spiritual forces are freed from their previous organic activities, and they flow into what I have called the body of formative forces, or the ether body. This member of the human being is entirely linked to the external world, and it is right for the child to live in it during the time between the change of teeth and puberty. If already before the change of teeth there were an excess of these etheric forces, that is, if the child has lived too much in its etheric sheath before the second dentition, the outcome is a markedly phlegmatic temperament. However, it is quite possible for a child to have a normal and balanced relationship with the etheric body, and this is absolutely essential between the seventh and the fourteenth years, that is, between the change of teeth and puberty. Again, if this condition is carried over too far into later life, a decidedly phlegmatic temperament will develop in the grown-up.

The next member of the human being which, under normal circumstances gains its independent existence in puberty and which yesterday I called the astral body—the member of the human being which lives beyond space and time—is the real birthplace of the sanguine temperament. And if, during the time between the change of teeth and puberty, a child draws too much upon what should come into its own only when sexual maturity is reached, the sanguine temperament comes into being. Only with the arrival of puberty does the growing human being become inwardly mature for sanguinity. Thus, everything in life has its right or normal period of time. The various abnormalities come about if that which is normal for one particular time of life is pushed into another period of life. If you can survey life from this viewpoint, you learn to understand the human being in depth.

And now, what is actually happening during the time of sexual maturity? Our considerations of the last few days have already shed some light on it. We have seen how, after the change of teeth, the child is still working inwardly with those forces which, to a certain degree, have become emancipated soul and spiritual forces. During the subsequent stages the child incarnates via the system of breathing and blood circulation to where in the tendons the muscles grow onto the bones. It incarnates from within outwards towards the human periphery, and at the time of sexual maturity, the young adolescent breaks through into the external world. Only then does she or he fully stand in the world.

This dramatic development makes it imperative for the teacher to approach the adolescent, who has passed through sexual maturity, quite differently from the way in which he has dealt with him or her prior to this event. For, fundamentally, the previous processes involving the emancipated soul and spiritual forces before puberty had as yet nothing to do with sex in its own realm. True, boys or girls show a definite predisposition towards their sexes, but this cannot be considered as actual sexuality. Sexuality only develops after the breakthrough into the external world, when a new relationship with the outer world has been established.

But then, at this particular time, something is happening within the realm of the adolescent's soul and bodily nature which is not unlike what happened previously during the second dentition. During the change of teeth forces were liberated to become actively engaged in the child's thinking, feeling, and willing, forces which were directed more towards memory. The powers of memory were then released. Now at puberty something else becomes available for free activity in the soul realm. These are powers which previously had entered the rhythms of breathing and which, subsequently, were striving to introduce rhythmical qualities also into the muscular and even into the bony systems.

This rhythmical element now becomes transmuted into the adolescent's receptiveness for all that belongs to the realm of creative ideas, for all that belongs to fantasy. Fundamentally speaking, genuine powers of fantasy find their birth only during puberty, for they can come into their own only after the astral body has been born. It is this same astral body which exists beyond time and space and which links together past, present, and future according to its own principles, as we can experience it in our dreams.

What is it that the adolescent brings with him when he "breaks through" into the external world via his bony system? It is what originally he had brought down with him from pre-earthly existence and what, gradually, had become interwoven with his whole inner being. And now, with the onset of sexual maturity, the adolescent is being cast out of the spiritual world, as it were. Without exaggerating, one can really put it that strongly, for it represents the actual truth; with the coming of puberty the young human being is cast out from the living world of the spirit and thrown into the external world which he or she can perceive only by means of the physical and etheric bodies. And though the adolescent is not at all aware of what is going on inside him, subconsciously this plays an all the more intensive part. Subconsciously, or semi-consciously, it makes the adolescent compare the world he has now entered with the world which he formerly had within himself. Previously he had not experienced the spiritual world consciously, but, nevertheless, he had found it possible to live in harmony with it. His inner being felt attuned to it and ready to cooperate freely with the soul and spiritual realm. But now, in these changed conditions, the external world no longer offers such possibilities to him. It presents all kinds of hindrances which, in themselves, create the wish to overcome them. This, in turn, gives rise to the tumultuous relationship between the adolescent and the surrounding world, lasting from the fourteenth or fifteenth year until the beginning of the twenties.

This inner upheaval is bound to come, and it is well for the teacher to be aware of it already during the previous years. There may be people of an unduly sensitive nature who believe that it would be better to save teenagers from such inner turmoil, only to find that they have made themselves their greatest enemy. It would be quite wrong to try to spare them this tempestuous time of life. It is far better to plan ahead in one's educational aims so that what has been done with the pre-puberty child can now come to the help and support of the adolescent's soul and spiritual struggles.

The teacher must be clear that with the arrival of puberty an altogether different being emerges, born out of a new relationship with the world. It is no good appealing to the pupil's previous sense of authority, for now he demands to know reasons for whatever he is expected to do. The teacher must get into the habit of approaching the young man or woman rationally. For example, if the adolescent who has been led by the spiritual world into this earthly world becomes rebellious because this new world is so different from what he had expected, the adult must try to show him— and this without any pedantry—that everything he meets in the world has a prehistory. He must get the adolescent to see that present conditions are the consequences of what has gone on before. One must act the part of the expert who really understands why things have come to be as they are. From now on, one will accomplish nothing by way of authority. Now one has to be able to convince the adolescent through the sheer weight of one's indisputable knowledge and expertise and by giving him waterproof reasons for everything one does or expects of him. If, at this stage, the pupil cannot see sound reasons in all the content given to him, if conditions in the world appear to make no sense to him, he will begin to doubt the rightness of his previous life. He will feel himself in opposition with what he experienced during those years which, apparently, only led him into these present unacceptable outer conditions. And if, during his inner turmoil, he cannot find contact with people who are able to reassure him, at least to a certain extent, that there are good reasons for what is happening in the world, then the inner stress may become intolerable to the extent that the adolescent breaks down altogether. For this newly emerged astral body is not of this world. The young person has been cast out of the astral world, and he is willing to place himself into this earthly world only if he feels convinced of its rightful existence.

You will completely misunderstand what I have been describing if you think that the adolescent is at all aware of what is thus going on within him. During his ordinary day consciousness it rises up from the unconscious in dim feelings. It is surging up through blunted will impulses. It lives itself out in the disappointment of apparently unattainable ideals, in frustrated desires, and perhaps also in a certain inner dullness towards what presents itself out there in the unreasonable happenings of the world.

If, during this stage, education is to be effective at all—and this indeed must be the case for any youngster willing to learn—then the teaching content must be transmitted in the appropriate form. It must also be a preparation for the years to come, up to the early twenties or even later in life. Having suffered the wounds inflicted by life and having paid back in his own coinage, the young person of fifteen to twenty-one or twenty-two eventually will have to find his way back again into the world from which he has been cast out during puberty. (The duration of this period varies, especially so during our chaotic times which tend to prolong it even further into adult life.) The young person must feel accepted again; he must be able to make a new contact with the spiritual world, for without it, life is not possible. However, should he feel any coercion coming from those in authority, this new link will lose all meaning and value for life.

If we are aware of these difficulties already well before the arrival of puberty, we will make good use of the child's inborn longing for authority in order to bring it to the stage when there is no longer any need for an authoritarian approach. And this stage should coincide with the coming of sexual maturity. But by then the educator must always be ready and able to give convincing reasons for everything he wishes his pupil to do. Seen from a wider, spiritual perspective, we can thus observe the grandiose metamorphosis which is taking place in the human being during the period of sexual maturity.

It is of the greatest importance to realize that the whole question of sex becomes a reality only during puberty, when the adolescent enters the external world in the way I have described it. Naturally, since everything in life is relative, this, too, has to be taken as a relative truth. Nevertheless, one has to recognize that up to the stage of sexual maturity, the child lives more as a general human being, and that an experience of the world, differentiated according to whether one lives as a man or woman, only begins with the onset of puberty. This realization—which in our generally intellectual and naturalistic civilization cannot be taken for granted—will allow people who, without prejudice, are striving for a knowledge of man, a real insight into the relationship between the sexes. It also helps them to understand the problem regarding the position of women in society, not only during our present times but also in the future.

Only if one can appreciate the tremendous metamorphosis which is taking place in the male organism during voice maturation—to mention just one example—will one be able to understand fully the statement that up to the age of sexual maturity the child retains a more general human character, as yet undivided into sexes. Other similar processes occur also in the female organism, only in a different area. The human voice with its ability to moderate and to form sounds and tones is a manifestation of man's general human nature. It is born out of the soul and spiritual substance which is working upon the child up to puberty. Changes of pitch and register, on the other hand, occurring during maturation, are the result of external influences. They are forced upon the adolescent from outside, as it were. They are the means by which he places himself into the outer world with his innermost being. It is not only a case of the soft parts in the larynx relating themselves more strongly to the bones, but a slight ossification of the larynx itself takes place which fundamentally amounts to a withdrawal of the larynx from the purely human inner nature into a more earthly existence.

This stepping out into the world should really be seen in a much wider context than is usually the case. Usually, in people's minds, the capacity to love, which awakens at this time, is directly linked to sexual attraction. But this is by no means the whole story. The power to love, born during sexual maturity, embraces everything within the adolescent's entire compass. Love between the sexes is but one specific and limited aspect of love in the world. Only by seeing human love in this light can one understand it correctly, and then one also understands its task in the world.

We may well ask: What is really happening in a human being during the process of sexual maturity? Prior to this stage, as a child, his relationship to the world was one where he first imitated the surroundings and when, subsequently, he stood under the power of authority. Outer influences were working upon him for, at that time, his inner being mainly represented what he had brought down with him from pre-earthly life. Humanity as a whole had to work upon him from without, first through the principle of imitation and then through authority. But now, at puberty, having found his own way into humanity and no longer depending on its outer support to the same extent that a pre-puberty child does, there rises up in him a new feeling, an entirely new appraisal of mankind as a whole. It is this new experience of humankind which represents the spiritual counterpart to the physical faculty of reproduction. Physically he becomes able to procreate. Spiritually he becomes capable of experiencing mankind as a totality.

During this new stage, the polarity between man and woman becomes very marked. Only through a real understanding of the other sex by means of social intercourse, also in the realm of soul and spirit, is it possible for the human potential to come to some kind of realization on earth. Both man and woman fully represent humankind, but each in a differentiated way. The woman sees in humanity a gift of the metaphysical worlds. Fundamentally, she sees humanity as the result of a divine outpouring. Unconsciously and in the depths of her soul she bears a picture of mankind which acts as her standard of values, and she evaluates and assesses mankind according to this standard. If these remarks are not generally accepted today, it is due to the fact that our present civilization shows all the signs of a male-dominated society.

For a long period of time the most powerful influences in our civilization have displayed a decidedly masculine character. An example of this—however grotesque it may sound—can be found in freemasonry. It is symbolic of our times that men, if they wish to keep certain matters to themselves, separate themselves off into lodges of freemasonry. There are also lodges in which both men and women congregate, but in these, freemasonry has already become blunted, and they no longer bear its original stamp. The constitution of freemasonry is, of course, a specific example, but it is, nevertheless, indicative of the male-dominated character of our society. Women, too, have absorbed a great deal of the masculine element in our civilization, and because of this they are actually preventing the specifically feminine element from coming into its own. This is the reason why one so often gains the impression that, with regard to inner substance and outer form, there is hardly any difference between the ideals and programs of the various women's movements and those of men, even to the very tone of speeches in which they are delivered. Obviously these movements are different from each other insofar as on the one side demands are made to safeguard women's interests, while on the other they are made on behalf of men, but with regard to inner substance, they are scarcely distinguishable from each other.

Man, in his innermost being, experiences humanity as something of an enigma. To him it appears as something unfathomable which poses endless questions, the solutions of which seem to lie beyond his powers. This typically masculine characteristic expresses itself in all the mysterious ceremony with its dry and manly atmosphere which belongs to freemasonry. This same male tendency has permeated our culture to such an extent that, on the one hand, the women are suffering under it and, on the other, they are wanting to emulate it, wishing to make it part of their lives too.

If you take a good look at modern medicine with all its materialistic features, if you see how it fails to comprehend human nature, especially with regard to its physical aspect, so that it depends on experimentation, and if you observe modern medicine, you will find there the product of a distinctly masculine attitude, however strange this may sound to you. In fact, one could hardly find a better illustration of male thinking than in what modern medicine so blatantly reveals to us.

If one expounds the truth today, people tend to think that one does so merely for the sake of putting paradoxical statements into the world. Yet the reality is often paradoxical. Therefore, if one wishes to speak the truth, one has to put up with appearing paradoxical, however inconvenient this may be.

While womankind lives more in the image it creates of humanity, man's experiences of humanity are more of a wishful and enigmatic kind. In order to understand this situation, one needs to become clear about one other symptom of our times, which is of particular significance for the art of teaching: When people speak about love today, they do not generally differentiate between the various kinds of love. Of course, one can generalize about the concept of love, just as one can speak about condiments in a general way. But if someone puts abstract speculations about certain matters into the world and then holds forth about them, it always strikes me as if he were talking about salt, sugar, or pepper merely in terms of condiments. He only needs to apply such abstractions to practical life by putting salt into his coffee instead of sugar—because, after all, both are condiments—to realize his foolishness. Anyone who indulges in general speculations instead of entering the concrete realities of life commits the same folly.

A woman's love is very different from that of a man. Her love originates in the imaginative realm, and it is constantly engaged in making pictures. A woman does not love a man just as he is, standing there before her in ordinary humdrum life—forgive me for saying this but, after all, men are not exactly of the kind a healthy imagination could fall in love with—but she weaves into her love the ideal she has received as heaven's gift. Man's love, on the other hand, is tinged with desire; it is of a wishful nature. This differentiation needs to be made, no matter whether it shows itself more in an idealistic or a realistic sense. Ideal love may inspire longings of an ideal nature. The instinctive and sensuous kind may be a mere product of fancy. But this fundamental difference between love as it lives in a man or a woman is a reality. A woman's love is steeped in imagination. In man's love there is an element of desire. It is just because of this complementary character that the two kinds of love can become harmonized in life.

An educator should bear this in mind when confronted with pupils who have already passed through the stage of sexual maturity. He should realize that by that time it is no longer possible to bring to them certain things which belong to the pre-adolescent stage and that the opportunity for doing so has been missed. Therefore, in order to prevent a one-sided attitude in later life, one must endeavor to give to pre-puberty children enough of the right content to last them through the coming stages.

In our times when, fortunately, coeducation in both primary and secondary education is accepted more and more readily so that boys and girls work side by side in order to learn how to cooperate as men and women in social life later on; it is of special importance to pay heed to what has just been said. Through it, a contemporary phenomenon, such as the women's movements, will be placed upon a really sound and healthy basis.

During our previous meetings I already mentioned that really one ought to throw away all school textbooks, because only the direct and personal relationship of teacher to pupil should work upon the child. But when it comes to teaching adolescents, all available textbooks and, for that matter, almost our entire outer civilization, become one great source of pain. I know that there are many people who are unaware of this, because they do not enter real life with sufficiently open eyes. But here again in this outer civilization we find a marked and one-sidedly masculine character. Any book on history, on the history of civilization or anthropology will confirm this trend. As representative of Western civilization, man longs to escape from the physical world in which he is caught up, but he lacks the courage to do so. He cannot find the bridge from the sense-perceptible world to the spiritual world. And so we find everywhere in our civilization a yearning to get away from it all and yet, at the same time, an inability to act accordingly.

It is hard enough to achieve the right outer conditions for teaching children of pre-puberty age. But anyone who has to teach adolescents could almost feel helpless because the means available for meeting their needs are so totally inadequate. This fact alone should kindle a real longing in their teachers for deeper insight into the human being. This longing may, of course, be there already in teachers of younger children, but it is a prerequisite for anyone of sound pedagogical sense who is teaching adolescents.

A woman's nostalgia for the ways of the East and a man's wish to free himself from the bondage of Western life represent a fundamental feature of our times. This differentiation between the sexes is less apparent in pre-adolescent children who still bear more general human features. Yet as soon as we are confronted by adolescents, we meet the resulting difficulties quite concretely.

Let us assume, for example, that a teacher of German literature wanted to recommend a book about Goethe—as seen from a German point of view—to an adolescent pupil. He really would find himself in a quandary, for there simply are no suitable books on the market. If he chose one of the available ones, his scholar would not gain the right picture of Goethe. If he chose a biography of Goethe written by, let us say, Lewes, a German scholar would learn to know the more outward features of Goethe better than from any of the German books on the subject, but again he would not become acquainted with the specifically German characteristics of Goethe. This is the general situation today, for we simply do not have an adequate literature for teaching adolescents.

To remedy this situation, everything will depend on the women taking their proper place in our cultural life. They should be allowed to contribute their specifically feminine qualities, but, at the same time, they must be careful not to introduce anything they have adopted from our male-oriented civilization.

Whenever we, as teachers, approach the growing human being, we must be aware of the striking contrast between pre-puberty and post-puberty years. Let us take a concrete example: There is Milton's *Paradise Lost*. It would be good to use it in our lessons. The question is, when? Those of you who have thought over what has been said so far and who have understood my remarks about the right time for introducing the narrative and descriptive element, will find that this work by Milton—as all epic poetry in general—would become suitable material after the tenth year. Also Homer will be appreciated best if taught between the tenth and the fourteenth years. On the other hand, it would be premature to use Shakespeare as study material already at this stage for, in order to be ready for dramatic poetry, the pupil must at least have entered puberty. To absorb the dramatic element at an earlier age would mean that the pupils concerned would have to drive something out of themselves prematurely, something which, later on, they would definitely miss.

What I tried to indicate just now can be experienced vividly if one has to give, for example, history lessons to boys and girls after their entry into puberty. Both masculine and feminine forces were at work during the actual historical happenings, though in a different form from that of today. Yet all historical accounts available for teaching adolescents bear a decidedly masculine quality, as if they had been compiled by Epimetheus. Girls who have reached sexual maturity show little inclination towards such an approach. Boys may find it somewhat boring, but in their case it is not impossible to use this Epimethean way, which is one of judging, of holding on to what can be ascertained and established.

But there is also a Promethean way of looking at history which does not only record the events that actually occurred, but also shows their metamorphosis into ideas current at the present time. This latter approach to history shows how impulses which led the past have become current ideas of the present, and how impulses, in turn, continue to lead present times further. This Promethean way of looking at history appeals especially strongly to the feminine element.

However, it would be very one-sided to teach history in the Promethean style in a girls' school and in an Epimethean style in a boys' school. The minds of the young men would simply flow back into past times to become even more rigid than they are already. If only the Promethean way of teaching history were to be applied in a girls' school, the pupils would feel tempted to fly off into futuristic speculations. Everywhere they would feel attracted to those impulses for which they happened to have a natural liking. We will also achieve a more balanced social life only if we add to the Epimethean way, which up until now is practically the only one available, a historical outlook bearing the prophetic marks of Prometheus. Then, if both attitudes are alive in our lessons, we shall at last achieve the right approach to history for pupils who have reached the age of sexual maturity.

One can characterize the astral body from many different aspects, and one of them is based on what happens in the human being during the development of sexual maturity. If one observes the relevant phenomena and their underlying forces, one will arrive at a picture of the astral body, because puberty is the time of its birth, the time when it can be freely used by the human being.

St. Augustine, the medieval writer, tried to approach the human astral body in yet another way. Here I wish to point out that in his writings one finds a description of man's invisible members which is still in agreement with the one given in anthroposophy. His findings, however, were the outcome of an instinctive clairvoyance, once the common heritage of all mankind, and not the result of a conscious investigation into the spiritual realm, as practiced in anthroposophy. The way in which St. Augustine describes the astral body becoming independent at puberty is truly characteristic of human life. He says it is due to the fundamental properties of the astral body that the human being is able to become acquainted with everything of a man-made origin which affects human life. If we build a house, make a plough, or invent a spinning machine, we do so by making use of forces which are directly bound to the astral body. It is a fact that the human being learns with his astral body to know everything which is the product of human activities within his surroundings. It is, therefore, fully consistent with a true knowledge of man if we, as educators, introduce the adolescent to the practical sides of life which represent the results of human ingenuity. This, however, is a far more complicated process today than in St. Augustine's times, when life was altogether simpler. Only by applying what, during previous lectures, I called "soul-economy in teaching" can we hope to succeed in planning an education for pupils aged fifteen to twenty, or even older, which will gradually introduce them to the manifold contrivances surrounding them today. Just think for a moment of how much we fall short of this task in our present civilization. You only need to ask yourselves how many people there are who regularly use the telephone, the tramway, or even a steamship without having the faintest idea of how they work. In our civilization people are almost engulfed by a technology which they do not understand. Those who believe that only our conscious experiences are of real importance will dismiss these remarks as irrelevant. Certainly, it is easy enough to enjoy life consciously if one is satisfied with buying a tram ticket in order to be set down at the place of one's choice, or if one receives a telegram without having any idea of how the message ever reached the recipient, without having the slightest notion of what a Morse apparatus is like. The ordinary consciousness is unconcerned about whether it understands the processes or not, and from this point of view, it is arguable enough whether these things matter or not. But if one looks at what is happening in the depths of the unconscious, the picture looks entirely different. Anyone who uses products of modern technology without having any knowledge of how they work or of how they were made is like a person in a prison cell without a window through which he would at least be able to look out into nature, into freedom.

Educators ought to be fully aware of this fact. With the adolescent's experience of the differentiation between the sexes, the time is ripe for the understanding of yet other differentiations in modern life. The pupil now needs to be introduced to the practical aspects of life, and this is the reason why, with the approach of puberty, we include crafts, such as spinning and weaving, in our curriculum. Naturally, such a plan brings many difficulties in its wake, certainly from the timetable point of view. When planning our curriculum, we must also bear in mind the demands of other training centers, such as universities, technical colleges, or other similar institutions, to which our pupils may wish to gain entry. This, in turn, makes it imperative for us to include some subject matter which, in our opinion, is of lesser value for life. It really causes us a great deal of trouble and pain to achieve a balanced curriculum which is entirely dependent on strict soul economy in teaching. It is a most difficult task, but not an impossible one.

It can be achieved if the teacher develops a sense of what is of real importance for life and if he is capable of getting it across to his pupils in the most economical and simplified ways, so that eventually they will learn to know what they are doing when using a telephone, a tram, or any other modern invention. We must aim at making our pupils familiar with the ways of our present civilization, so that they can see sense in it. Already before the age of puberty the teacher has to prepare his chemistry and physics lessons in such a way that, after the onset of puberty, he can build upon what was given and extend it to become the basis for an understanding of the practical spheres of life.

Here we must consider yet another point, namely that the pupils are now entering an age when, at least to a certain extent, they need to be grouped according to whether they will follow a more academic or a practical career later on. At the same time we must never forget that an education based on a true knowledge of man will always strive for balance in teaching, for teaching the whole man. What is needed here is the knowledge of how to achieve this in practice. Naturally, we must equip pupils of a more academic disposition with what they will need for their future schooling. At the same time, in order to retain a proper balance, any specialization—also during later ages—should be compensated for by some widening out into otherwise neglected areas. If on the one hand we direct the pupils' will impulses more towards the academic side, we must give them also some concrete insights into practical life, so that they will not lose sight of life as a totality. In this way we are actually fulfilling the demands of the human astral body which, when it guides conscious will impulses in a certain direction, at the same time feels the need for appropriate counter impulses.

To give a concrete example: It would be quite wrong—to quote an extreme case—if a statistician were to spend his time making statistics of the consumption of soap in certain districts without having the slightest notion of how soap is manufactured. No one can arrive at a proper understanding of such statistics unless he has at least some general knowledge of how soap is made in factories.

Those of our pupils who are likely to follow an academic career should gain at least some experience of practical work involving manual skills. On the other hand, pupils who are likely to take on an apprenticeship for a trade should become acquainted also with the kind of background needed for the more academic types of professions. All this should be part of the general school curriculum. It is not right to send boys and girls straight into the factories to work there alongside grownup workers. Instead the various crafts should be introduced at school, so that the young people can use what they have learned there as a kind of model before they find their way into more professional skills. Nor do I see any reason why older pupils should not be given the task of manufacturing certain articles in school workshops to be sold on the open market. This has already been achieved in some of our prisons, where prisoners' products are being sold outside.

A young person should remain within a school setting for as long as possible, provided that life at school is both constructive and healthy. For it is in keeping with the inner nature of the human being to enter life gradually and not to be flung into it too early and all of a sudden. It is just because the older generation has shown so little understanding of the needs of the younger generation that there exists today such a strong international youth movement, the justification of which is understood least of all by the older people. There are deep reasons for the emergence of this movement, which ought to be not only recognized but also guided into the right channels. This, however, is only possible if the principles of education, too, are guided into the right channels.

One of the main objectives of Waldorf education is to fit the students for life as far as this is possible, so that when a young person reaches the early twenties—when his ego enables him to take his full share in social life—he can develop the right relationship to the world at large. At that time, young people should be able to feel a certain kinship with their elders; for, after all, it was their generation which provided the wherewithal used by the young generation. The young folk should feel appreciation of and understanding for the achievements of the older generation. Thus, when sitting in a chair, they should not only realize that the chair was made by someone belonging to the generation of their fathers, but they should also know something about how it was made.

And when we turn to the life of feeling, we find there something which takes us out of ourselves, which leads us out into the surrounding world. When experiencing gratitude, we find ourselves confronting other beings. But if we can identify ourselves with other beings to the extent of experiencing them as ourselves, then something begins to develop in our feeling life which we call love in the true sense of the word. Love is the second mood of soul which needs to be nurtured with regard to the ethical and religious life. It is the kind of love which we can foster at school by doing everything we can so that the pupils will love each other. It is the kind of love to which we can give a firm grounding by aiding the children's gradual transition from the stage of imitation and that of authority between their ninth and tenth years to a genuine feeling of love for their teachers, whose bearing and general behavior at school naturally must warrant it.

In this way we lay the foundations of a twofold human quality: on the one hand we implant what is contained in the ancient call, "Love thy neighbor as thyself." Since at the same time we are also developing a feeling of gratitude which points more to a comprehension of the world, "Love thy neighbor as thyself" is complemented by the words, "Love the Divine Being above all things."

Such words of truth have a familiar ring to most people today, for they have been sounding across the ages.

However, to know them in theory and to repeat them is not the point. What matters is that in our immediate present, and every age sees a renewal of mankind, we find ways and means of putting them into practice. Nowadays one hears all too often, "Love thy neighbor as thyself and God above all things." Yet one sees little evidence of it. Life at school should help to bring about that such things are not merely talked about, but that they become infused with new life.

There is only one way which will offer a firm foundation for a mature capacity to love, and that is the natural transformation of the childhood stages of imitation and authority to that of love. And if we work in harmony with the child's natural development towards the attainment of love, the quality of which should be self-evident when seen in this context, we no longer need to invent long-winded theories of the kind that are fabricated by materialistic thinkers with the intention of guiding the newly sexually mature adolescent in his first experiences of love. A whole literature has been written on this subject, all of which suffers from the simple fact that one no longer knows what to do with youngsters when they reach sexual maturity. And the reason for this failure lies in the children not having been prepared adequately for this event because one did not know how to handle the previous stages of childhood. If adolescents have been guided rightly up to this incisive time in their lives, one does not have the same difficulties with them.

Soul Economy and Waldorf Education.
Hudson, N.Y.: Anthroposophic Press, 1986.

Authority

When the child has outgrown the stage of authority, when he has attained puberty and through this has physiologically quite a different connection with the outer world than before, he also attains in soul and body (in his bodily life in its most comprehensive sense) a quite different relationship to the world than he had earlier. This is the time of the awakening of spirit in humanity. This now is the time when the human being seeks out the rational and logical aspect in all verbal expression. Only now can we hope to appeal with any success to the intellect in our education and instruction. It is immensely important that we do not consciously or unconsciously call upon the intellect prematurely, as people are so prone to do today.

And now let us ask ourselves: What is happening when we observe how a child takes on authority, everything that is to guide and lead his soul? For a child does not listen to us in order to check and prove what we say. Unconsciously the child takes up as an inspiration what works upon his soul, what, through his soul, builds and influences his body. And we can only rightly educate when we understand the wonderful, unconscious inspiration which holds sway in the whole life of a child between seven and fourteen, when we can work into the continuous process of inspiration. To do this we must acquire still another power of spiritual cognition we must add inspiration itself to intuition. And when we have led the child on his way as far as the fourteenth year we make a peculiar discovery. If we attempt to give the child things that we have conceived logically, we become wearisome to him. To begin with he will listen, when we thus formulate everything in a logical way; but if the young man or maiden must rethink our logic after us, he will gradually become weary. Also in this period we, as teachers, need something besides pure logic. This can be seen from a general example.

Take a scientist such as Ernst Haeckel who lived entirely in external nature. He was himself tremendously interested in all his microscopic studies, in all he built up. If this is taught to pupils, they learn it, but they cannot develop the same interest for it. We as teachers must develop something different from what the child has in himself. If the child is coming into the domain of logic at the age of puberty, we (in our turn) must develop imagery, imagination. If we ourselves can pour into picture form the subjects we have to give the children, if we can give them pictures, so that they receive images of the world and the work and meaning of the world, pictures which we create for them, as in a high form of art—then they will be held by what we have to tell them.

So, in this third period of life we are directed to imagination, as in the other two to intuition and inspiration. And we now have to seek for the spiritual basis which can make it possible for us as teachers to work from out of imagination, inspiration and intuition—which can make it possible not merely to think of spirit, but to act with spirit.

And when the child has passed the age of puberty—the age in which young ladies and gentlemen come into full possession of their own minds, their own spirits—he enters upon the age in which we must no longer speak of him as a child. Thus, man progresses from what is of the body, by way of the soul, into the spiritual. But, as we shall see, we cannot teach what is of the spirit. It has to be freely absorbed from the world. Humans can only learn of spiritual things from life.

If we now turn to the moral aspect, the question is how we can best get the child to develop moral impulses? Here we are dealing with the most important of all educational questions. Now we do not endow a child with moral impulses by giving him commands, by saying: You must do this, this has to be done, this is good, or by wanting to prove to him that a thing is good and must be done. Or by saying: That is bad, that is wicked, you must not do that, and by wanting to prove that a certain thing is bad. A child has not as yet the intellectual attitude of an adult towards good and evil, towards the whole world of morality. He has to grow up to it. And this he will only do on reaching puberty, when the rhythmic system has accomplished its essential task and the intellectual powers are ripe for complete development. Then the human being may experience the satisfaction of forming moral judgment in contact with life itself. We must not engraft moral judgment onto the child. We must so lay the foundation for moral judgment that when the child awakens at puberty he can form his own moral judgment from observation of life.

The last way to attain this is to give finite commands to a child. We can achieve it, however, if we work by examples, or by presenting pictures to the child's imagination: for instance through biographies or descriptions of good men or bad men; or by inventing circumstances which present a picture, an imagination of goodness to the child's mind. Since the rhythmic system is particularly active in the child during this period, pleasure and displeasure can arise in him, not judgment as to good and evil, but sympathy with the good which the child beholds presented in an image or antipathy to the evil which he beholds so presented. It is not a case of appealing to the child's intellect, of saying, "Thou shalt" or "Thou shalt not," but of fostering aesthetic judgment, so that the child shall begin to take pleasure in goodness, shall feel sympathy when he sees goodness, and feel dislike and antipathy when he beholds evil. This is a very different thing from working on the intellect, by way of precepts formulated by the intellect. For the child will only be awake for such precepts when it is no longer our business to educate him, namely, when he is a man and learns from life itself. And we should not rob the child of the satisfaction of awakening to morality of his own accord. And we shall not do this if we give him the right preparation during the rhythmic period of his life; if we train him to take an aesthetic pleasure in goodness, an aesthetic dislike of evil, if here, also, we work through imagery.

Otherwise, when the child awakens after puberty he will feel an inward bondage. He will not perhaps realize this bondage consciously, but throughout his subsequent life he will lack an important experience: morality has awakened within me, moral judgment has developed. We cannot attain this inner satisfaction by means of abstract moral instruction; it must be rightly prepared by working in this manner for the child's morality.

If we have received the child in religious reverence, if we have educated him in love up to the time of puberty, then our proper course after this will be to leave the youth's spirit free, and to hold intercourse with him on terms of equality. The aim is not to touch the spirit but to let it be awakened. When the child reaches puberty, we shall best attain our aim of giving the child over to free use of his intellectual and spiritual powers if we respect the spirit and say to ourselves: You can remove hindrances from the spirit, physical hindrances and also, up to a point, hindrances of the soul. What the spirit has to learn it learns because you have removed the impediments. If we remove impediments, the spirit will develop in contact with life itself even in very early youth. Our rightful place as educators is to be removers of hindrances.

Hence, we must see to it that we do not make the children into copies of ourselves, that we do not seek forcibly and tyrannically to perpetuate what is in ourselves in those who in the natural course of things develop beyond us. Each child in every age brings something new into the world from divine regions, and it is our task as educators to remove bodily and physical obstacles out of his way, to remove hindrances so that his spirit may enter in full freedom into life. These then must be regarded as the three golden rules of the art of education, rules which must imbue the teacher's whole attitude and all the impulse of his work. The golden rules which must be embraced by the teacher's whole being, not held as theory, are: Reverent gratitude to the world in the person of the child which we contemplate every day, for the child presents a problem sent to us by divine worlds. Thankfulness to the universe. Love for what we have to do with the child. Respect for the freedom of the child—a freedom we must not endanger; for it is to this freedom we educate the child, that he may stand in freedom in the world at our side.

Among girls, in certain circumstances, you will find a slight tendency to chlorosis, to anemia, in the whole developing organism. The blood in the girl's organism becomes poor; she becomes pale, anemic. This is due to the fact that during these fourteenth, fifteenth and sixteenth years the spiritual nature is separated out from the total organism; and this spiritual nature, which formerly worked within the whole being, regulated the blood. Now the blood is left to itself. Therefore, it must be rightly prepared so that its own power may accomplish this larger task. Girls are apt, then, to become pale, anemic, and one must know that this anemia comes about when one has failed to arouse a girl's interest in the things one has been teaching or telling her. Where attention and interest are kept alive, the whole physical organism participates in the activity which is engaging the inmost self of the human being, and then anemia does not arise in the same way.

With boys the case is opposite. The boys get a kind of neuritis, a condition in which there is too much blood in the brain. Hence, during these years the brain behaves as though it were congested with blood. In girls we find a lack of blood in the body, in boys a superabundance, particularly in the head—a superabundance of white blood, which is a wrong form of venous and arterial blood. This is because the boys have been given too many sensations, they have been over-stimulated and have had to hurry from sensation to sensation without pause or proper rest. And you will see that even the troublesome behavior and difficulties among fourteen-, fifteen- and sixteen-year-old children are characteristic of this state and are connected with the whole physical development.

When one can view the nature of the human being in this way, not despising what is physical and bodily, one can do a great deal for the children's health as a teacher or educator. It must be a fundamental principle that spirituality is false the moment it leads away from the material to some castle in the clouds. If one has come to despising the body, and to saying the body is a low thing, it must be suppressed, flouted, one will most certainly not acquire the power to educate men soundly. For, you see, you may leave the physical body out of account, and perhaps you may attain a high state of abstraction in your spiritual nature, but it will be like a balloon in the air, flying off. A spirituality not bound to what is physical in life can give nothing to social evolution on the earth, and before one can wing one's way into the Heavens one must be prepared for the Heavens. This preparation has to take place on earth.

I alluded yesterday to what takes place when the boys and girls one is educating come to be fourteen- or fifteen-year olds and reach puberty. At this stage, a teacher who takes his responsibilities seriously will encounter many difficulties. And these difficulties are particularly apparent in a school or college where the education is derived from the nature of man. Now, it is out of the question to overcome these difficulties by extraneous discipline. If they are repressed now they will only reappear later in life in all manner of guises. It is far better to look them squarely in the face as an intrinsic part of human nature and to deal with them. In a school like the Waldorf school where boys and girls are educated together and are constantly in each other's company such difficulties occur very frequently.

We have already referred to the difference between boys and girls which begins to appear about the tenth year. At this age girls begin to grow more vigorously and, particularly, to shoot up in height. Boys' growth is delayed until around puberty. After that, the boys catch up with the girls. For one who observes the fine interplay between spirit, soul and body from the standpoint of a true human knowledge, this is of great significance. Growing, the overcoming of the earth's gravity by growth, engages the fundamental being of man, his essential manhood, whereas it is not essentially a concern of the human being whether a certain organic phenomenon appears at one stage or another of this life. Actually, certain cosmic, extra-human influences, which work in upon the human being from the external world, affect the female organism more intensely between the tenth and twelfth years than they do the male organism. In a certain sense the female organism between the tenth and twelfth years partakes even bodily of the supersensible world.

Please realize the importance of this: Between the tenth and twelfth years, or the thirteenth and fourteenth, the female organism begins to dwell in a spiritual element. It becomes permeated by spirit at this period. And this affects the processes of the blood in girls in a very special way. During these years the blood circulation is, as it were, in contact with the whole universe. It must take its time from the whole world, from the universe, and be regulated by it. And experiments carried out to find the relationship between the rhythm of pulse and breath between ten and twelve years, even if done with external instruments, would find the results among girls other than among boys.

The boy of thirteen or fourteen begins to show a nature hitherto unrevealed, and now he begins to grow more than the girls do. He grows in all directions. He makes up for the delay in his growing. At the same time his relationship to the outer world is quite other than it was in the earlier periods of his life. And so in boys it is the nervous system which is now affected, rather than the circulation of the blood. Thus, it can easily happen that the boy's nervous system gets overstrained if the instruction at school is not given him in the right way. For in these years, the form and content of language, or of the languages he has learned, have an enormous influence upon him. The ideas of men enshrined in language, or in foreign languages, press upon the boy, beset him as it were, while his body grows more delicate. And so at this age the whole world drones and surges within a boy—the world, that is, of this earthly environment.

Thus, in girls a year or two sooner is implanted something of the surrounding universe; in boys earthly environment is implanted through the medium of language. This is apparent externally in the boy's change of voice. And indirectly, in connection with this transformation in the voice enormously important things take place in the boy's whole organism. In the female organism, this rounding off of the voice is very slight. On the other hand in connection with the quickened growing, there has been a preparation in the organism, which is, as it were, a flowing into the maiden of supernal worlds. The recent advances of materialistic science of the world come into their own spiritual view.

When you have the attitude of a Waldorf teacher towards the children, you tend to look in quite a different way upon a child who has reached puberty, a child who has just passed through that stage of development which includes the organic changes I have alluded to. You look upon this child in quite a different way from that of a person who knows nothing of all this, who knows nothing of it, that is, from the spiritual point of view.

A boy of fourteen or fifteen years old echoes in his being the world around him. That is to say: Words and their significant content are taken up unconsciously into his nervous system, and they echo and sound in his nerves. The boy does not know what to do with himself. Something has come into him which begins to feel foreign to him now that he is fourteen or fifteen. He comes to be puzzled by himself, he feels irresponsible. And one who understands human nature knows well that at no time and to no person, not even to a philosopher, this two-legged being of the Earth called Anthropos seems so great a riddle as he does to a fifteen-year-old boy. For at this age all the powers of the human soul are beset by mystery. For now the will, the thing most remote from normal consciousness, makes an assault upon the nervous system of the fifteen- or sixteen-year-old boy.

With girls it is different. But when we aim, as we should aim, at equal treatment for both sexes, at an equal recognition, a thing which must come in the future, it is all the more important to have clearly in view the distinction between them. So, now, whereas for the boy his own self becomes a problem, and he is perplexed by himself, for girls at this time the problem is the world about them. The girl has taken up into herself something not of the earth. Her whole nature is developing unconsciously within her. And a girl of fourteen or fifteen is a being who faces the world in amazement, finding it full of problems; she is above all, a being who seeks in the world ideals to live by. Thus, many things in the outer world become enigmatic to a girl at this age. To a boy the inner world presents many enigmas. To a girl it is the outer world.

One must realize, one must come to feel, that one now has to deal with quite new children—not the same children as before. And this change in each child comes, in some cases, remarkably quickly, so that a teacher not alive to the transformation going on in the children in his charge may fail to perceive that he is suddenly confronting a new person.

You see, one of the most essential things in the training of the Waldorf school teachers themselves is receptivity to the changes in human nature. And this the teachers have acquired relatively quickly for reasons which I shall explain. A Waldorf teacher—if I may express myself paradoxically— has to be prepared to find a thing completely different to-morrow from what it was yesterday. This is the real secret of his training. For instance, one usually thinks in the evening: Tomorrow the sun will rise and things will be the same as they are today. Now—to use a somewhat drastic mode of expression which brings out my meaning—the Waldorf teacher must be prepared for the sun not to rise one day. For only when one views human nature afresh like this, without prejudice from the past, is it possible to apprehend growth and development in human beings. We may rest in the assurance that things out there in the universe will be somewhat conservative. But when it is a case of that transition in human nature from the early years of childhood into the fourteenth, fifteenth and sixteenth years, why then, ladies and gentlemen, the sun that rose earlier often does not rise. Here, in this microcosm, Man, in this Anthropos, so great a change has come about that we face an entirely new situation, as though nature upon some day should confront us with a world of darkness, a world in which our eyes were of no use.

Openness, a readiness to receive new wisdom daily, a disposition which can subdue past knowledge to a latent

feeling which leaves the mind clear for what is new—it is this that keeps a man healthy, fresh and active. And it is this open heart for the changes in life, for its unexpected and continuous freshness, which must form the essential mood and nature of a Waldorf teacher.
Spiritual Grounds of Education.
London: Rudolf Steiner Press, 1976.

True Knowledge—Eighteen- and Nineteen-Year-Olds

Now let us suppose that a three-year-old child were to resolve not to pass through the tedious process of waiting for its second teeth until the seventh year, but this child were to say: It is weary work to go through four more years until I get my second teeth; I will get them at once. (I could use other comparisons which would appear still more grotesque, but this one will suffice.) Such a thing is impossible, is it not? For there are certain conditions of natural development.

And so, too, it is a condition of natural development, for which today only few people have any feeling, that only from a certain age onwards the human being can know something about the connections in life of which he must know, but which cannot be exhausted by information about external things. Naturally even at the age of nine we may know, for example, that the human being has ten fingers. But matters where judgment formed by active thinking is necessary cannot be known before we reach a certain time in life, that is, between about the eighteenth and nineteenth years. Just as it is impossible to get the second teeth before the seventh year, so it is impossible to know something in its essential reality before the eighteenth year. It is simply impossible before the eighteenth year really to know about those things that are not just under our noses, things for which active judgment is necessary. Before this one may have heard something, may believe something on authority. But one cannot know anything about it. Before this we cannot unfold that inner activity of soul necessary for us to say: I know something about this or that which does not lie in a region accessible to mere eyes or ears. Such things are hardly mentioned today. They are, however, exceedingly important for life. If culture is to find roots again, one must speak about such things and treat them in a knowledgeable way.

What, then, follows from the fact that before his eighteenth year the human being cannot, properly speaking, know anything? It follows that the human being before he is eighteen must depend upon those who are older, just as the infant is dependent on his mother's breast—it is in no way different.

One answer to this question is found by learning to perceive—for it is a matter of the unfolding of will and not of a theoretical solution—that when the child enters earthly existence, he brings with him the power of imitation; up to the time of the change of teeth, the child just imitates. Out of this power of imitation speech is learned. Speech is, so to speak, poured into the child just as his blood circulation is poured into him when he comes into earthly existence. But the child should not come to a more and more conscious education by giving him, out of consciousness-soul, knowledge in the form of truth. In earlier times it was said: Before the eighteenth year the child cannot know anything, so he must be led through ability to knowledge which he accepts first as belief; thereby the forces of knowledge will be awakened in him between the eighteenth and nineteenth years. For it is out of the inner being that the forces of knowledge must be awakened. To keep the young waiting until their eighteenth year, adults behaved in relation to youth so as to show what they were capable of, afterwards educating them to experience together with the teacher in a provisional way, up to the eighteenth year, what later they would be expected to know. Up to the eighteenth or nineteenth year the "acquisition of knowledge" was provisional, because before the eighteenth or nineteenth year it is not possible really to know anything. But in fact no teacher can convey knowledge to any boy or girl if in their feeling there has not ripened the conviction: He is capable! A teacher has not the right sense of responsibility towards the human being if he wants to set to work before the young take it as a matter of course that he knows his job.

Science does not leave the human being alone even in earliest childhood. It cannot very well be otherwise. For the teacher is so drilled in systematized botany (and many books are entirely given over to systematized botany) that he believes he is committing a sin if he speaks to the children about botany in a way that is not scientific. But what is found in a botanical textbook cannot mean anything to a child before he is ten, and it is not until he is at least eighteen or nineteen that it can acquire any real significance for him.

Such is the situation. Now I have no intention of creating another intellectual theory about education. The aim is to create an artistic atmosphere between the older and the younger. But when this comes about, something happens which must occur if young people are to grow into the world in a healthy way. What the human being of today grows into can be described quite concretely. Between the ninth and tenth years an undefined feeling lives in the soul of every human being who is not a psychopath. There need not necessarily exist either a clear or unclear concept of this. But it begins to live within the human being from his ninth or tenth year. Up until then what is called the astral body alone is concerned with man's life of soul. But from that time onwards the force of the ego nature first begins to stir. It is not formulated in concepts. But in the life of feeling, deep within the soul, there lives unconsciously a question in the heart of the growing human being. This question takes different forms in different people. But a question arises which put in the form of a concept might be expressed as follows: Up to now the astral body has believed in other human beings; now I need something that somebody says to me so that I may believe in him or in others in my environment. Those who as children have most resisted this are those who need it most. Between the ninth and tenth years the human being, to strengthen his ego, begins to be dependent on an older person in whom he can trust—without this trust needing to be drummed in—in whom he can believe with the help of the artistic atmosphere that has been created. And woe betide him if this question which may still be one for many children up to their sixteenth or seventeenth year and sometimes even to the years I mentioned yesterday, the eighteenth or nineteenth—woe betide him if nothing happens to enable this question of the young to be answered by the old so that the young say: I am grateful that I have learned from the old what I can learn only from the old; what he can tell me, he alone can tell me, for it will be different if I learn it when I am old.

Through this can be created something in an educational way which, applied in the right way, can be of the greatest significance for the epoch of the consciousness soul, which, in fact, in the earliest times of the Patriarchs, was already alive between young and old. Then, every young person said to himself: The old man with his snow-white hair has experiences which can only come when one is as old as he. Before then the necessary organs are not there. Therefore, he must tell his experiences to us. We are dependent on what he relates, because he alone can relate it. Certainly I shall one day be as old as he. But I shall not experience what he tells for thirty-five or forty years. The times will have progressed by then and I shall experience something different. But what I want to learn is only to be learned from him.

Before puberty it is preeminently an experience of the pre-earthly. The pre-earthly sheds its light through every movement of the hands, every look, through the very stressing of words. Actually, it is the quality of the gesture, the word, the thought, of the teacher that works through to the child and which the child is seeking.

And when as grown-up people—so grown-up that we have reached the age of fifteen or sixteen or even beyond—we meet other human beings, then the matter is still more complicated. Then what attracts or repels others in a human being actually veils itself in a darkness impenetrable to the world of abstract concepts. But if, with the help of anthroposophy, we investigate what one can really experience in five minutes but cannot describe in fifty years, we find that it is what rises up from the previous earth-life or series of earth-lives into the present life of the soul and what is exchanged. This indefinite, indefinable element that comes upon us when we meet as adults is what shines through from earlier lives on earth into the present, not only the pre-earthly existence but everything the human being has passed through in the way of destiny in his successive earth-lives.

The Younger Generation.
Hudson, N.Y.: Anthroposophic Press,
1967.

The Transition from Childhood into Adolescence

When the child has reached puberty, the astral body, which has been working through language up to this point, now becomes free—free to work independently. Previously, the forces working through the medium of language were needed for the building up of the inner organization of the child's body. But after puberty, these forces, which are also working in many other spheres—in all that is form-giving, both with regard to plastic and musical forms—these manifold forces are becoming liberated, to be used for the activity of thinking. Only now does the young person become an intellectualizing and logically thinking person.

One can clearly see how what is thus flashing, streaming, and surging through language delivers a final jolt to the physical body before becoming liberated. Look at a boy of this age and listen to how his voice changes during puberty. It is a change equally as decisive as the change of teeth in the seventh year. When the larynx begins to speak with a different undertone of voice, it is the last jerk the astral body, that is, the forces flashing and working through speech, makes in the physical body. A corresponding change also occurs in the female organism, only in a different way and not in the larynx. It is brought about through other organs. Having undergone these changes, the human being has become sexually mature.

And now the young person enters that period of life when what previously radiated into the body from the nerve-sense system is no longer the determining factor. Now it is the motor system, the will system, so intimately connected with the metabolic system, that takes over the leading role. The metabolism lives itself out in physical movements. Pathology in adults can show us how at this later age illnesses radiate out predominantly from the metabolic system. (Even migraine is a metabolic illness.) We can see how in adults illnesses no longer spread from the head, as they do in children. It does not matter so much where an illness manifests itself. What matters is to know the source from which it radiates out into the body.

Only when the transition from the second life-period to the third takes place is the possibility given for—how shall I call them now in these modern times?—the young men and the young women to observe the activities going on around them. Previously it was the meaningful gesture that was perceived, and later the meaningful language of the events around the child. Only now does the possibility exist for the adolescent to observe the activities performed by other people in the environment. I have also said that out of the perception of meaningful gestures, and through the experience of gratitude, the love of God develops, and that through the meaningful language coming from the surroundings, love for all things human is developed as the foundation for the individual's sense of morality. If now the adolescent is enabled to observe other people's activities in the right way, love of work will develop. While gratitude must be allowed to grow and love must be awakened, what is to evolve now must make its appearance with the young person's full inner awareness. We must have enabled him or her to enter this new phase of development after puberty with full inner awareness, so that in a certain way the adolescent comes to find the self. Then love of work will develop. This love of work has to grow freely on the strength of what has already been attained. It is love of work in general and also love for what one is doing oneself. At the moment when an understanding for the activities of other people awakens, a conscious attitude towards love of work, "love of doing," must arise as a complementary image. In this way, during the intervening stages, the child's early play has become transmuted into the right conception of work, and this is what we must aim for in our society today.

Instructions to Teachers

What part do teachers and educators have to play in all this? It is something that belongs to one of the most difficult things in their vocational lives. For the best thing they can do for the child during the first and second life-periods is to aid what will awaken out of its own accord with the advent of puberty. When, to their everlasting surprise, they witness time and again how the child's individuality is gradually emerging, they have to realize that they themselves have been only a tool. Without this attitude, sparked off by this realization, one can hardly be a proper teacher. For in one's classes one is faced with the most varied types of individualities, and it would never do to stand in one's classroom with the feeling that all one's pupils ought to become copies of oneself. Such a sentiment should never arise. And why not? Because it could well happen that, if one is fortunate enough, among one's pupils there might be three or four budding geniuses, quite apart from the dull ones, about whom we will have to speak later. You surely will admit that it is not possible to select only geniuses for the teaching profession, and that it is bound to happen that teachers are not endowed with the genius that some of their pupils will display in later life. Yet teachers must be able to educate not only pupils of their own caliber but also those who, with their exceptional brightness, will far outshine them.

However, this the teachers will be able to do only if they get out of the habit of hoping to make their pupils into what they themselves are. If they can make a firm resolve to stand in the school as selflessly as possible, and to obliterate not only their own sympathies and antipathies but also their personal ambitions, in order to dedicate themselves to all that comes from the pupils, then they will rightly educate potential geniuses as well as dull-witted pupils. Only such an attitude will lead to the realization that all education, fundamentally, is a matter of self-education.

Basically, there is no education other than self-education, whatever the level may be. In its full depth this is recognized in anthroposophy, which through spiritual investigation has conscious knowledge of repeated earth lives. Every education is self-education, and as teachers we can only provide the environment for the child's own self-education. We have to provide the most favorable conditions in which, through our agency, the child can educate himself in accordance with his own destiny.

This is the attitude the teacher should have towards the child, and it can be developed only through an ever-growing awareness of this fact. For people in general there may be many kinds of prayers. Over and above these there is this special prayer for the teacher:

> *Dear God, make that I, as far as my personal ambitions are concerned, quite obliterate myself. And Christ make true in me the Pauline word—Not I, but the Christ in me.*

This prayer, addressed to God in general and to Christ in particular, continues: ". . . that the Holy Spirit may hold sway in the teacher." This is the true Trinity.

If one is able to live in these thoughts while in close proximity to the pupils, then the hoped-for results of this education can at the same time also become a social deed. But here other matters, too, come into play, and I can only touch upon them. Just consider what in the opinion of many people would have to be done in order to improve today's social order. They expect better conditions through the implementation of external measures. You need only look at the dreadful experiments that are being carried out in Russia. There the happiness of all the world is sought through the inauguration of external programs. It is believed that improvements in the social sphere depend on the creation of institutions. And yet, these are the least significant factors within social development. You can set up any institutions you like, be they monarchist or republican, democratic or socialist. The decisive factor will always be the kind of people who live and work under any of these systems. And for those who spread a socializing influence, the two things that matter are a loving devotion towards what they are doing, and an understanding interest in what the others are doing.

Think about what can flow from just these two attributes. With nothing less than that, people can again work together in the social sphere. But this will have to become a tradition over eons. As long as you work only externally, you will produce no tangible results. You have to bring out these two qualities from the depths of human nature. If you want to introduce changes by external means, even if these are set up with the best of intentions, you will find that people will not respond in the way expected. And, conversely, their actions may elude your own understanding. Institutions are the outcome of individual endeavor—you can see this everywhere. They were brought into being by the very two qualities which, to a greater or lesser extent, lived in the initiators, namely loving devotion to what they were doing, and an understanding interest in what the others were doing.

If one looks at the social ferment in our times with open eyes, one will find that the most peculiar ideas have arisen, especially in the social sphere, simply because the present situation was not understood properly. Let me give you an example.

Today, the message of so-called Marxism regarding human labor and its relationship to social relationships is being drummed not just into thousands but into millions of heads. And if you investigate what its author alleges to have discovered—something with which millions of people are being indoctrinated so that they look upon it as their socialist gospel, to use as a means for political agitation—you will find that it all rests upon a fundamental error regarding the attitude towards social realities. Karl Marx wants to base the value of work done on the human energy spent while performing it. This leads to a complete absurdity. For from the point of view of energy output, it makes no difference whether someone cuts a certain quantity of firewood within a given time or whether—if he can afford to avoid such a menial task—he spends his energy and time on treading down the pedals of a wheel specially designed to combat incipient obesity. According to Karl Marx's reckoning there is no difference between the human energy expended on those two physical activities. But cutting firewood has its proper place within the social order. Treading the pedals of a slimming wheel, on the other hand, is of no social use, because it only provides a hygienic effect for the person doing it. And yet, Karl Marx's yardstick for measuring the value of work consists of calculating the food consumption necessary for work to be done. This way of assessing the value of labor within the context of the national economy is simply absurd. Nevertheless, all kinds of calculations were made towards this end. But the importance of one factor was ignored, namely loving devotion towards what one is doing and an understanding interest in what others are doing.

What we must achieve when in the company of the young is that by our own conduct a full consciousness of the social implications contained in those two sentences will enter the minds of the adolescents. To do so we must realize what it means to stand by the child in such a way that we aid his own self-education.

Now, to come back to our point, after the twelfth year it becomes increasingly difficult to find a workable compromise with regard to our way of teaching. Up to the twelfth year it is just possible to do so, so long as one really knows what is going on inside the pupils. But afterwards the situation begins to get more and more difficult, because from that time on, the curricula and the required standards of achievement no longer have any connection with what corresponds to the nature of the growing human being; they are chosen entirely arbitrarily. The subject matter to be covered in any one year is chosen entirely autocratically, and one simply can no longer bridge the conflicting demands made, on the one hand, by the powers that be, and, on the other, by what springs directly from the evolving human being. Remember what I said yesterday, by the time puberty is passed, the adolescent ought to have been helped towards developing sufficient maturity and inner strength to enter the realm of human freedom. I referred to the two fundamental virtues—gratitude, for which the ground has to be prepared before the change of teeth, and the ability to love, for which the ground needs to be prepared between the change of teeth and puberty—this theme was developed yesterday.

Furthermore, we have seen that, with regard to the life of ethics, the soul life of the child must also experience feelings of sympathy and antipathy towards what is good and evil. If one approaches a pupil of this age with a "thou shalt" attitude, one will hinder the right development in the years to come. On the other hand, if instead, through natural authority, one moves the pre-pubescent child to love the good and hate the evil, then during the time of sexual maturity, out of the inner being of the adolescent, there develops the third fundamental virtue, which is the sense of duty. It is impossible to drill it into young people. It can only unfold as part of natural development, and this only on the foundation of gratitude—in the sense described yesterday—and on the ability to love. If these two virtues have been developed rightly, when sexual maturity is reached, the sense of duty will emerge, the experience of which is an essential part of life. For what belongs to the realm of the human soul and spirit has to develop according to its own laws and conditions, just as what belongs to the realm of the physical has to obey the physical laws. Just as an arm or a hand has to be allowed to grow freely, that is, in accordance with the inner forces of growth, just as these must not be artificially controlled by, say, being fixed into a rigid iron frame—although in certain regions of the earth there is a custom of restricting the free growth of feet in a way similar to that in which we, here, impede the free unfolding of the child's soul life—so must the adolescent feel that this new sense of duty is arising freely from within. Then the young person will integrate him or herself rightly into society, and Goethe's dictum will find its noblest fulfillment. "Duty is to love what one commands oneself to do." Here again you see how love plays into everything, and how the sense of duty has to be developed in such a way that eventually one comes to love it. In this way one properly integrates oneself as a human being into society. And then, from the previous experience of right authority, the ability of supporting oneself on one's own strength will evolve.

What finally reveals itself as genuine piety, when seen with spiritual eyes, is the transmuted, body-linked, natural religiousness during the time before the change of teeth, as I have described it to you in fair detail. These are all things that have to be deeply rooted in a true pedagogy and its practical application. Soon enough, one will realize how necessary it is to let the curriculum, from the twelfth year until puberty, and, above all, after puberty, tend more and more towards practical activities. In the Waldorf school the ground for this task is already prepared early on. In our school, boys and girls sit side by side. Although interesting psychological facts have emerged from this practice alone—and each class has its own psychology, of which more tomorrow—one can definitely say: if one lets boys and girls practice their handicrafts sitting side by side as a matter of course, it is an excellent preparation for their adult lives. Today there are but few men who recognize how much help towards healthy thinking and healthy logic can be derived from the ability to knit. Only a few men can judge what it means for one's life if one is able to knit. In our Waldorf school, boys do their knitting alongside the girls, and they also mend socks. Through this practice, the differentiation between the types of work performed by the two sexes will find its natural course later on, should this become necessary. At the same time, a form of education is being implemented that takes full account of the practical aspects of the pupils' future lives.

People are always terribly surprised when they hear me say—and the following assertion not only expresses my personal conviction but is based upon a psychological fact— I cannot consider anyone to be a good professor in the full meaning of the word unless he or she is also capable of mending a shoe in an emergency. For how could it be possible for anyone to know something of real substance about being and becoming in the world, unless such a person can also repair a shoe or a boot if the situation demands it? This is, of course, rather a sweeping statement, but there are men who cannot even sew on a trouser button properly, and this is a lamentable failing. Knowledge of philosophy carries little weight, unless one is also able to turn a hand to anything that needs doing. This is simply part of life. In my opinion, one can only be a good philosopher if one could equally well have become a shoemaker, should this have been one's destiny. And, as the history of philosophy shows, it sometimes happens that cobblers become philosophers.

Knowledge of the human being calls upon us to make adequate provision in our curricula and schedules for preparing pupils for the practical side of life. Reading in the book of human nature, we are simply led to introduce the children—or rather, the young men and women, as we should call them now—to the art of weaving and of setting up a loom. From there it follows quite naturally that they should also learn to spin, and that they gain a working idea of how paper is manufactured, for instance. They should be taught not only mechanics and chemistry, but also how to understand at least simple examples of mechanical and chemical processes used in technology. These they should reproduce on a small scale with their own hands, so that they will know how various articles are manufactured. This change of direction towards the more practical side of life must definitely be made possible. It has to be striven for with honest and serious intentions, if one wishes to build up the right curriculum, specifically for the upper classes.

But this can land one in terrible difficulties. It is just possible to equip children under nine with sufficient learning skills for a transfer into Class IV of another school, without neglecting what needs to be done with them for sound pedagogical reasons. This is also still possible in the case of twelve year olds who are to enter Class VII. It is already becoming very difficult indeed to bring pupils to the required standards of learning for their transfer to a Gymnasium or Realschule. But tremendous difficulties have to be overcome if pupils from our upper classes have to change to one or the other of these senior schools.

In such cases one would do well to recall the days of ancient Greece, where a wise Greek had to put up with being told by an Egyptian, "You Greeks are like children—you know nothing about all the changes the earth has gone through." A wise Greek had to listen to the judgment of a wise Egyptian. But nevertheless, the Greeks had not become so infantile as to demand of a growing youth, who was to be educated in one or another particular subject, that he should first acquire knowledge of the Egyptian language. They were quite satisfied with his using his native Greek tongue. Unfortunately, today we do not act as the Greeks did, for we make our youngsters learn Greek. I do not wish to speak against it; to learn Greek is something beautiful. But it is inconsistent with fulfilling the needs of a particular school age. It becomes a real problem when one is told to allocate so many lessons to this subject on the schedule at a time when such a claim clashes with the need for lessons in which weaving, spinning, and a rough knowledge of how paper is made ought to be practiced. Such is the situation in which one is called upon to finalize the schedule! And since we know only too well that we shall never be granted permission to build up our own university anywhere, it is absolutely essential for us to enable those of our pupils who wish to continue their education at a university, technical college, or other similar institution, to pass the necessary graduation exam (Arbitur).

All this lands us in an almost impossible situation, with almost insuperable difficulties. While one is trying to cultivate the practical side in education, prompted by insight into the inner needs of adolescent pupils, one has to face the bitter complaints of a Greek teacher who declares that he could never cover the exam syllabus with the lesson time allocated to his subject, and that, in consequence, his candidates are doomed to fail in their exams.

Such are the problems we have to tackle. They surely show that it is impossible for us to insist on pushing through our ideals with any fanatical fervor. What will eventually have to happen no longer depends solely on the consensus of a circle of teachers regarding the rights and wrongs of education. Today it has become necessary for much wider circles within society to recognize the ideals of a truly human education, so that outer conditions will make it possible for education to function without alienating pupils from life. For this is obviously the case if, after having gone through a grammar school type of education in one's own school, pupils were to fail their graduation exams, which they have to take somewhere else.

Speaking of failing an exam—and here I am speaking to specialists in education—I do believe that it would be possible to make even a professor of botany, however clever he might be, fail in his own subject—if such were one's only intention! I really believe such a thing to be possible, for anyone could fail in an exam. In this chapter of life, also, some most peculiar facts have come to light. There lived, for instance, a Robert Hamerling, an Austrian poet, whose use of the German language was later acclaimed the highest level any Austrian writer could possibly reach. The results of his exam certificate, qualifying him for a teaching position at an Austrian Gymnasium, make interesting reading: Greek—excellent; Latin—excellent; German language and essay writing—hardly capable of teaching this subject in the lower classes of a middle school. You actually find this written in Hamerling's teaching certificate! So you see, this matter of failing or passing an exam is quite a tricky business.

And so the difficulties besetting us make us realize that society at large must provide better conditions before one can achieve more than what is possible making the kind of compromise of which I have spoken. If I were to be asked, quite abstractly, whether a Waldorf school could be opened anywhere in the world, I could only answer, again entirely in the abstract, "Yes, wherever one would allow it to be opened." On the other hand, even this would not be the determining factor for, as already said, in the eyes of many people these are but two aspects of one and the same thing. There are some who struggle through to become famous poets, despite having bad exam results in their main subject. But not everyone is able to do so. For many, a failed graduation exam means being cast out of the stream of life. And so it has to be admitted that the higher the class in our school, the less one is able to work towards all one's educational ideals. It is something not to be lost sight of. It shows how one has to reckon with actual life situations.

For an education based on an understanding of the human being, the following question has to be ever-present. Will the young people, as they enter life, find the right human contact in society, which is one of the fundamental human needs? For, after all, those responsible for the demands made in graduation exams are members of society, too, even if the style and content of their exam papers is based upon error. And so, if one wishes to integrate Waldorf pedagogy into our present social conditions, one has to put up with having to do certain things that in themselves one would not consider right or beneficial. Anyone inspecting our top classes may well be under the impression that what is found there does not fully correspond to the avowed ideals of Waldorf pedagogy. But I can guarantee you that if we were to carry these out regardless of the general situation—and especially where we attempt to make the transition to the practical side of life—all our candidates for the graduation exam would fail! So diametrically opposed do matters stand today. But they have to be reckoned with, and this can be done in the most varied ways. At the same time an awareness has to emerge of how much needs to be changed, not only in the field of education, but in life in general, before a truly human form of education becomes established.

Despite all obstacles, the practical activities are being carried through in the Waldorf school, at least to a certain level—even if it does happen, from time to time, that in some cases they have to be curtailed because the Greek or Latin teacher claims some of these lessons. It is something that cannot be avoided.

From the foregoing you will have seen that puberty is the right time to make the transition, leading the adolescent into the realities of outer life. And that those elements will have to play more and more into school life that, in a higher sense, will make the human individual, as a being of body, soul, and spirit, a helpful and useful member of society. In this respect our present period lacks the necessary psychological insight, for the finer interrelationships in the human spiritual, soul, and physical spheres are generally not even dreamt of. These can be felt intuitively only by people who make it their special task to learn to know the human psyche. From personal self-knowledge I can tell you in all modesty that I should not have been able to accomplish certain things in spiritual science in the way this proved possible if, at a particular time in my life, I had not learned bookbinding—which may well appear to be of little use to many a person. And this was not in any way connected with Waldorf pedagogy, but simply as part of my destiny. This particularly human activity is of special consequence to most intimate spiritual and soul matters, especially if it is practiced at the right time of life. The same also holds true for other practical activities. I should consider it a sin against human nature if we did not include bookbinding and box-making in our Waldorf school craft lessons, introduced into the curriculum at a particular age determined by insight into the pupil's development. These things are all part and parcel of becoming a full human being. What matters in this case is not the fact that a pupil has made a particular cardboard box, or that she or he has bound a book, but that the pupils have undergone the discipline necessary in making such items, and that they have experienced the inherent feelings and thought processes that go with them.

The natural differentiation between the boys and girls will become self-evident. Yet here also one needs to have an eye for what is happening, an eye of the soul. For instance, the following situation has arisen, the psychology of which has not yet been fully investigated because I have been unable to spend enough time at the Waldorf school. It will be gone into thoroughly at a later date. What has happened is that during lessons in spinning, it was the girls who took to the actual spinning. The boys, too, wanted to be involved, and somehow they found their task in fetching and carrying for the girls. The boys wanted to be chivalrous. They brought the various materials the girls then used for spinning. The boys seemed to prefer doing the preparatory work. This is what happened, and we still need to digest it from the psychological point of view.

But this possibility of "shunting our craft lessons about"—if I may put it thus—allows us to switch, now to bookbinding and then to box-making. All are part of the practical activities which play such a dominant role in Waldorf pedagogy, and which show how an eye for the practical side of life is a natural by-product for anyone who has made spiritual striving and spiritual research the main objective in life. There are educational methods in the world, the brain-child of downright unpractical theoreticians who believe they have eaten practical life experience by the spoonful, methods that are, nevertheless, totally removed from reality. If one begins with educational theories, one will end up with the least practical results. Theories in themselves yield nothing useful, and all too often they breed only prejudices. A realistic pedagogy, on the other hand, is the offspring of a true knowledge of the human being. And the part played by arts and crafts at a certain time of life is nothing but such knowledge applied to a particular situation. In itself this knowledge already presents a form of pedagogy that will turn into the right kind of practical teaching through the living way in which the actual lessons are given. It becomes transmuted into the teacher's right attitude, and this is what really matters. The nature and character of the entire school has to be in tune with it.

This has led to the situation where, quite recently, while other problems facing the anthroposophical cause were being dealt with, a memorandum was handed in by the pupils of the present top class in the Waldorf school. Those among them who were expecting to have to take their graduation exam had worked out a remarkable document, the deeper aspects of which will be appreciated only when the whole matter is seen in the right light. They had sent more or less the following memorandum to the Anthroposophical Society: "Since we are being educated and taught in the sense of the true human being . . ."—this they had somehow gleaned ". . . and since, in consequence, we cannot enter already existing types of colleges, we wish to make the following proposal to the Anthroposophical Society: that a new Anthroposophical college is to be founded in which we can continue our education." (No negative judgment regarding colleges in general is implied in this wording, although such judgments are frequently met with in present-day society.)

All this presents us with the greatest difficulties. But as you have made the effort to come here in order to find out what this Waldorf pedagogy is all about—something we know how to appreciate only too well—these problems should also be aired. Any sincere interest in what is willed in this education deserves a clear indication of all the difficulties involved.

So far, Waldorf pedagogy is being practiced only by the teachers of the one existing Waldorf school, and there we find that our difficulties increase the higher up in the school we go. I can only assume that in a college run along anthroposophical lines, they would be greater still. But since such a college is only a very abstract ideal, I can speak about it only hypothetically. It has always been my way to deal directly with the tasks set by life, and this is the reason why I can talk about this education only up to Class XII, for its opening is imminent. The kind of things that belong to a misty future must not take up too much of the time of persons standing in life, since it would otherwise only detract from the real tasks at hand.

All one can say is that the problems would increase substantially and that there obviously would be two kinds of difficulties. First, if we were to open a college, our exam results would not be recognized as proper qualifications, which means that successful candidates could not take up professional positions in life. They could not become medical doctors, lawyers, and so on, professions that in their present customary forms are still essential today. This presents one side of the problem. The other side would conjure up really frightening prospects, if certain hard facts did not offer relief from such anxieties. For, on the strength of the praiseworthy efforts made by our young friends, an association has actually been founded with the express aim of working towards the creation of such a college, to be based upon the principles of Waldorf pedagogy. The only reason why there is no need to feel thoroughly alarmed about the potential consequences of such an undertaking is that the funds to be raised by this association surely will not reach such giddy heights as to tempt anyone to think seriously about going ahead with the project. The underlying striving towards this aim is thoroughly laudable, but for the time being it is still beyond the realm of practicality. The real worry would come only if, for example, an American millionaire were to suddenly offer the many millions needed to build, equip, and staff such a college. The best one could do in such a situation would be to promote, en masse, the entire teaching staff of the Waldorf school to become the teachers of the new college. But then there would no longer be a Waldorf school!

I am saying all this because I believe that actual facts are far more important than all kinds of abstract arguments. While acknowledging that the idea of founding education, including college education, upon true knowledge of the human being represents a far-reaching ideal, we must not overlook the fact that the circle of those who stand firmly behind our ideals is an extremely small one. This is the very reason why one feels so happy about every move towards an expansion of this work, which might possibly gain further momentum through your welcome visit to this course. At the same time, one must never lose sight of all that must happen in order that the Waldorf ideal can rest upon really firm and sound foundations. This needs to be mentioned within the context of this course, for it follows from the constitution of the Waldorf school.

This will also lead one to see that if one brings up children in the light of the education spoken of here, one allows something to grow up in them that will outlast their childhood days, something that will continue to have an effect throughout their lives. For what is it you have to do when you grow old? People who do not understand human nature are incapable of judging how important certain impulses, which can be implanted only during childhood, are for life. At that tender age it is still possible for these impulses to be immersed into the soft and pliable organism of the child, still so open to the musical-formative forces. In later years the organism becomes harder, not necessarily physically, but at any rate tending towards psycho-bodily sclerosis. However, what one has absorbed through one's upbringing and education does not grow old. However old one may have become, one is still inwardly endowed with the same youthful element that was one's own from, say, the tenth to the fifteenth year. This element of youthfulness one always carries within. But it has to remain so supple and flexible that the now aged brain—perhaps already covered by a bald head—is capable of using it in the same way in which the formerly soft brain did. However, if a person's education has not aided this process, the result is the generation gap, which so often makes its appearance these days, and which is considered unbridgeable.

People sometimes say something that, in reality, is the opposite of what is actually happening. For instance, one often hears the remark, "Today the young do not understand the old, because old people no longer know how to be young with the young." But this does not represent the truth. Not at all. What is really happening is that the young generation expects the old generation to be able to make the right use of the physical organization which has grown old. In this, the young recognize something in the old that is different from their own condition, something that is not yet theirs. It is this quality that leads to the natural respect for old age. When young people meet an old person who is still capable of using an already bald head in the way a child uses its tousled head, they feel that they can receive something from the old generation, something that they cannot find in their contemporaries. This is how it ought to be.

We must educate the young so that they know how to grow old in the right way. It is the malaise of our times that the young, as they grow up, do not recognize in members of the old generation people who have aged rightly. Instead, they see in them merely childish individuals who have remained at the same level of development as the young generation. Because, due to their inadequate education, old people are unable to make proper use of their physical organization, they remain infantile. The expression "big kids" is really chosen with great ingenuity, for it implies that such persons lost the ability to get hold of their entire organism during the course of their lives. They can work only with the head, which is precisely what children or youngsters are meant to do. So the young respond by saying, "Why should we learn from them? They have progressed no further than we have; they are just as childish as we are." The point is not that old age is lacking in youthfulness, but that it has remained behind at too infantile a stage, and this is what causes the difficulties today. You see how sometimes expressions chosen with the best of will have the opposite meaning of what they are supposed to convey.

All these things must be seen in their proper light before education can be put back on its feet again. This has become more than necessary today. Forgive this somewhat drastic way of saying it, but in our intellectual age education really has been turned upside down.

Puberty and Music

In answer to a question regarding music lessons given to a girl of seventeen Rudolf Steiner said: The essential thing is what Herr Baumann has already presented to us. With the onset of puberty and during the years following it, a certain musical judgment takes the place of a previous feeling for music and of a general musical experience. The faculty of forming musical judgments emerges. This becomes very noticeable through the phenomenon characterized by Herr Baumann, namely that a certain self-observation begins to manifest itself, a self-observation of the pupil's own singing and, with it, the possibility of using the voice more consciously, and so on. This has to be cultivated methodically.

But at the same time, something else becomes very noticeable, namely that from this stage onward the natural musical memory begins to weaken a little with the effect that pupils have to make greater efforts in remembering music. This is something which has to be specially borne in mind during music lessons. Whereas prior to puberty the children's relationship to music was a spontaneous, natural one and, because of it, their musical memory was excellent, some of them now begin to encounter difficulties—not in taking in the music, but in remembering it. This needs to be seen to. One must try to go over the same music several times, not by immediate repetition, but intermittently.

Another characteristic sign just at this stage is that whereas previously the instrumental and vocal parts of a piece were experienced as a unity, after the sixteenth to seventeenth year they are listened to with clear discrimination. (From a psychological point of view there is a fine and intimate difference between these two ways of listening.) At this age musical instruments are listened to far more consciously. There is also a greater understanding for the musical qualities of the various instruments used. Whereas earlier the instrument appeared to join in with the singing, it is now heard as a separate part. Listening and singing become two separate, though parallel, activities.

This new relationship between singing and the appreciation of the part played by musical instruments is characteristic of this new stage, and the methods of teaching must be changed accordingly. What is important is not to introduce any music theory before this age. Music should be approached directly, and any theoretical observations a teacher may wish to make should come out of the pupils' practical experience of it. Gradually it should become possible for pupils of this age to make the transition towards forming musical judgments on a more rational basis.

What Herr Baumann indicated at the end of his contribution, namely that one can make use of the ways in which pupils express themselves musically for increasing certain aspects of their self-knowledge, is absolutely correct. For instance, in the Waldorf school we let the older pupils do some modeling, and there, right from the start, one can perceive individual characteristics in what they produce. (When you ask children to model something or other, their work will always display distinctly individual features.) But with regard to musical activities, only when the age of sixteen to

136

seventeen is reached can the teacher go into the pupils' more individual characteristics. Then, in order to avoid one-sidedness, it is right to deal with questions posed by too great an attraction for a particular musical direction. If pupils of that age should develop a passion for certain types of music, for instance if they are strongly drawn to Wagner's music—and in our times many young people slide into becoming pure Wagnerites almost automatically—then the teacher must try to counterbalance their tendency to be swept away by music in too emotional a way, instead of their developing an appreciation of the inner configuration of the music itself. This in no way implies any criticism of Wagner's music.

What happens in such a case is that the musical experience too easily slips into the emotional sphere and consequently needs to be lifted up again into the realm of consciousness. A musician will already notice this in the quality of a pupil's singing voice. If music is experienced too much in the realm of feeling, the voice will sound differently from that of a young person who listens more to the formation of the tones and who has a correct understanding of the more structural element in music.

To work toward a balanced musical feeling and understanding is of special importance at this age. Naturally, before puberty the teacher, who is still the authority, has not yet any opportunity to work in this way. After puberty it is no longer the teacher's authority that counts, but the weight of her or his musical judgments. Up to puberty, right or wrong is concurrent with what the teacher considers to be right or wrong. After puberty reasons have to be given, musical reasons, also. Therefore, it is very important to go deeply into the motivation of one's own musical judgments if there is an opportunity for continuing music lessons at this age.

The Child's Changing Consciousness and Waldorf Education.
London: Rudolf Steiner Press, 1988.

Between the Seventh and Fourteenth Years

In Greek education the Gymnast must be recognized as one who preserved the forces of childhood on into the second period of life between the seventh and the fourteenth or fifteenth years. The "child" must be preserved—so said the Greeks. The forces of childhood must remain in the human being to the time of earthly death; they must be conserved. The Greek educator, the Gymnast, has in general to foster what he could not but point to in the seven- to fourteen-year- old child before him as his nature-foundation, his inherited nature-foundation. Out of his spiritual wisdom he had to know how to judge this and preserve it. Evolution in the Middle Ages went beyond this, and, as a result, our present age developed. Only now does the position of a modern man within the social order become a matter of consciousness. This fact of conscious life can only come into being after the age of puberty has been reached, after the fourteenth or fifteenth year. Then there appears in the human being something which I shall have repeatedly to describe in the following lectures as the consciousness of the real nature of inner freedom in the being of man. Then, indeed, man "comes to himself." And if, as it sometimes happens today, human beings believe themselves to have reached this consciousness before the fourteenth or fifteenth year, before the age of puberty, this is only an aping of later life. It is not a fundamental fact. It was this fundamental fact, which appears after the age of puberty, that the Greek purposely sought to avoid in the development of the individual man. The intensity with which he invoked nature, the "child," into human existence, darkened and obscured full experience of this moment of consciousness after puberty. The human being passed through it in a dimmed consciousness, restrained by nature. The historical course of human evolution, however, is such that this is no longer possible. This conscious urge would burst forth with elemental, volcanic force after the age of puberty if attempts were made to hold it back.

138

During what we call the elementary school age, that is to say, between the seventh and fourteenth years, the Greek had to take into consideration the earliest nature-life of the child. We in our day have to take account of what follows puberty, of that which will be experienced after puberty in full human consciousness by the boy or girl whom we have been guiding for seven years. We may no longer suppress this into a dreamlike obscurity as did the Greeks, even the highest type of Greek, even Plato and Aristotle, who, in consequence, accepted slavery as a self-evident necessity. Because education was of such a kind that it obscured this all-important phenomenon of human life after puberty, the Greek was able to preserve the forces of early childhood into the period of life between the seventh and fourteenth years.

Just as the period of life at about the seventh year is significant in earthly existence on account of all the facts which I have described, so, similarly, is there a point in the earthly life of man which, on account of the symptoms which then arise in life, is no less significant. The actual points of time indicated are, of course, approximate, occurring in the case of some human beings earlier, in others later. The indication of seven-year-long periods is approximate. But round about the fourteenth or fifteenth year there is once more a time of extraordinary importance in earthly existence. This is the period when puberty is reached. But puberty, the emergence of the life of sex, is only the most external symptom of a complete transformation that has taken place in the being of man between the seventh and fourteenth years. Just as we must seek in the growth-forces of the teeth—in the human head—for the physical origin of thought that frees itself about the seventh year of life, and becomes a function of soul, so we must look for the activity of the second soul-force, namely feeling, in other parts of the human organism.

Feeling releases itself much later than thinking from the bodily nature, from the physical constitution of the human being. And between the seventh and fourteenth years the child's feeling-life is still inwardly bound up with its physical organization. Thinking is already free; feeling is still inwardly bound up with the body. All the feelings of joy, of sorrow and of pain that express themselves in the child still have a strong physical correlation with the secretions of the organs, the acceleration or retardation, speed or slackening of the breathing system. If our perception is keen enough, we can observe in these very phenomena the great transformation that is taking place in the life of feeling, when the outer symptoms of the change make their appearance. Just as the appearance of the second teeth denotes a certain climax of growth, so the close of the subsequent life-period— when feeling is gradually released from its connection with the body and becomes a soul function—is expressed in speech. This may be observed most clearly in boys. The voice changes; the larynx reveals the change. Just as the head reveals the change which lifts thinking out of the physical organism, the breathing system—the seat of the organic rhythmic activity—expresses the emancipation of feeling. Feeling detaches itself from the bodily constitution and becomes an independent function of soul. We know how this expresses itself in the boy. The larynx changes, and the voice gets deeper. In the girl different phenomena appear in bodily growth and development, but this is only the external aspect.

Anyone who has reached the first stage of exact clairvoyance already referred to, the stage of imaginative perception, knows—for he perceives it—that the male physical body transforms the larynx at about the fourteenth year of life. The same thing happens in the female sex to the etheric body, or body of formative forces. The change withdraws to the etheric body, and the etheric body of the female takes on—as etheric body—a form exactly resembling the physical body of the male. Again, the etheric body of the male at the fourteenth year takes on a form resembling the physical body of the female. However extraordinary it may appear to a mode of knowledge that clings to the physical, it is, nevertheless, the case that from this all important period of life onwards, the man bears within him etherically the woman, and the woman etherically the man. This is expressed differently in the corresponding symptoms in the male and female.

Now if one reaches the second stage of exact clairvoyance—it is described in greater detail in my books—if, beyond imagination, one attains to inspiration—the actual perception of the independently spiritual that is no longer bound up with the physical body of man—then one becomes aware how, in actual fact, in this important period round about the fourteenth and fifteenth years, a third human member develops into a state of independence. In my books I have called this third being the astral body, according to an older tradition. (You must not be jarred by expressions; words have to be employed for everything.) This astral body is more essentially of the nature of soul than the etheric body; indeed, the astral body is already of the soul and spirit. It is the third member of man and constitutes the second supersensible member of his being.

Up to the fourteenth or fifteenth year this astral body works through the physical organism and, at the fourteenth or fifteenth year, becomes independent. Thus, there falls upon the teacher a most significant task, namely to help the development to independence of this being of soul and spirit which lies hidden in the depths of the organism up to the seventh or eighth year and then gradually—for the process is successive—frees itself. It is this gradual process of detachment that we must assist, if we have the child to teach between the ages of seven and fourteen. And then, if we have acquired the kind of knowledge of which I have spoken, we notice how the child's speech becomes quite a different thing. The crude science of today—if I may call it so—concerns itself merely with the crude soul-qualities of the human being and speaks of the other phenomena as secondary sexual characteristics. To spiritual observation, however, the secondary phenomena are primary, and vice versa.

These metamorphoses, the whole way in which feeling withdraws itself from the organs of speech, are of extraordinary significance. And as teachers and educators it is our wonderful task—a task that really inspires one's innermost being—gradually to release speech from the bodily constitution.

All this, however, the way in which the legs are placed, the capacity to prolong the movement of the arms into dexterity of the fingers—all this is still an outer, physical manifestation of the will in the boy or girl, even after the fifteenth year. Only at about the twentieth year does the will release itself from the organism in the same way as feeling releases itself about the fourteenth year and thinking about the seventh year at the change of teeth. The external processes that are revealed by the freed thinking, however, are very striking and can readily be perceived; the change of teeth is a remarkable phenomenon in human life. The emancipation of feeling is less so; it expresses itself in the development of the so-called secondary sexual organs—their growth in the boy, the corresponding transformation in the girl— the change of voice in the boy and the change of the inner life-habits of the girl, and so forth. Here, the external symptoms of the metamorphosis in the human being are less striking. Feeling, therefore, becomes independent of the physical constitution in a more inward sense.

The outer symptoms of the emancipation of the will at about the twentieth or twenty-first year are still less apparent and are, therefore, practically unnoticed by an age like ours, which lives in externalities. In our time—in their own opinion—human beings are "grown up" when they have reached the age of fourteen or fifteen. Our young people will not recognize that between the fifteenth and twenty-first years they should be acquiring not only outer knowledge but developing inner character and, above all, the will. Even before the age of twenty-one they set up as reformers, as teachers, and instead of applying themselves to what they can learn from their elders, they begin to write pamphlets and things of that kind. This is quite understandable in an age that is directed to the externals of life. The decisive change that takes place about the twentieth or twenty-first year is hidden from such an age, because it is wholly of an inner kind. But there is such a change, and it may be described in the following way.

Up to his twenty-first year of life, approximately, of course, man is not a self-contained personality; he is strongly subject to earthly gravity, to the earth's force of attraction. He struggles with earthly gravity until about the twenty-first year. And in this connection, external science will make many discoveries that are already known to the "exact clairvoyance" of which I spoke yesterday.

In our blood, in the blood corpuscles, we have iron. Until about the twenty-first year, the nature of these blood corpuscles is such that their gravity weighs them down. From the twenty-first year onwards, the being of man receives an upward impulse from below; an upward impulse is given to all his blood. From the twenty-first year he sets the sole of his foot on the earth otherwise than he did before. This, indeed, is not known today, but it is a fact of fundamental importance for the understanding of the human being so far as education is concerned. From the twenty-first year onwards, with every tread of the foot there works through the human organism from below upwards a force which did not work before. Man becomes a being complete in himself, one who has paralyzed the downward-working forces by forces which work from below upwards, whereas before this age all the force of his growth and development flowed downwards from the head.

On the other hand, it is altogether our intention to enable our children to enter the life of the world in the right way. To achieve this we must lead over from physics and chemistry to various forms of practical work when the child has reached the fourteenth and fifteenth years. In the classes for children of this age, therefore, we have introduced hand-spinning and weaving, for through these things one enters intelligently into practical life. Our pupils learn spinning and weaving and get to know something of how these things are done in a factory. They should also have some knowledge of elementary technical chemistry, the preparation and manufacture of colors, and the like.

During their school life children ought to acquire really practical ideas of their environment. The affairs of ordinary life often remain quite unintelligible to many people today, because the teaching they receive at school does not lead over, at the right moment, from the essentially human to the practical activities of life and the world in general. In a certain direction this is bound to injure the whole development of the soul. Think, for a moment, of the sensitivity of the human body to some element in the air, for instance, which the organism cannot assimilate. In the social life of the world, of course, conditions are not quite the same. In social life we are forced to put up with many incongruities, but we can adapt ourselves, if at the right age and in the right way we have been introduced into them.

Just think how many people nowadays get into a tram without having the faintest idea of the principles governing its motion and mechanism. Or they see a railway every day and have absolutely no notion of the machinery of a locomotive! This means that they are surrounded on all hands by inventions and creations of the human mind with which they have no contact at all. It is the beginning of unsocial life simply to accept these creations and inventions of the mind of man without understanding them, in a general way, at any rate. At the Waldorf school, therefore, when the children are fourteen or fifteen years old, we begin to give instruction and actual experience in matters that play a role in practical life. This age of adolescence is nowadays regarded from a very limited, one-sided point of view. The truth is that at puberty the human being opens out to the world. Hitherto he has lived more within himself, but he is now ready to understand his fellow men and the things of the world. Hence, to concentrate before puberty on all that relates man to nature is to act in accordance with true principles of human development, but at the age of fourteen or

144

fifteen we must with all energy begin to connect the children with the creations and inventions of the human mind. This will enable them to understand and find their right place in social life. If educators had adhered to this principle some sixty or seventy years ago, the so-called "Social Movement" of today would have taken quite a different form in Europe and America. Tremendous progress has been made in technical and commercial efficiency during the last sixty or seventy years. Great progress has been made in technical skill, national trade has become world trade, and finally a world-economy has arisen from national economies. In the last sixty or seventy years the outer configuration of social life has entirely changed, yet our mode of education has continued as if nothing had happened. We have utterly neglected to acquaint our children with the practical affairs of the world at the time when this should be done—namely, at the age of fourteen or fifteen.

After puberty, when the child has reached his fifteenth or sixteenth year, a change takes place in his inner nature, leading him from dependence upon authority to his own sense of freedom and hence to the faculty of independent judgment and insight. Here is something that must claim our most watchful attention in education and teaching. If, before puberty, we have awakened the child's feeling for good and evil, for what is and is not divine, these feelings will arise from his own inner being afterwards. His understanding, intellect, insight, and power of judgment are uninfluenced; he can now form independent judgments from out of his own being.

If we start by telling the child that he ought to do this and ought to do that, it all remains with him through his later years, and then he will always be thinking that such and such a thing is right, and such and such a thing is wrong. Convention will color everything. Now in true education today, the human being should not stand within the conventional but have his own judgment even about morality and religion, and this will unfold naturally if it has not been prematurely engaged.

At the Waldorf school we allow the child of fourteen or fifteen to find his own feet in life. We put him really on a par with ourselves. He unfolds his judgment, but he still looks back to the authority which we represented and retains the affection he had for us when we were his teachers. His power of judgment has not been fettered, if we have merely worked upon his life of feeling. And so, when the child has reached the age of fourteen or fifteen, we leave his nature of soul and spirit in freedom and, in the higher classes, appeal to his own power of judgment and insight. This freedom in life cannot be achieved by inculcating morality and religion in a dogmatic, canonical fashion but by working simply and solely on the child's powers of feeling and perception at the right age—the period between the change of teeth and puberty. The great thing is to enable the human being to find his place in the world with due confidence in his own power of judgment. He will then feel and sense his complete manhood, because his education has been truly and completely human. If someone has been unfortunate enough to have lost a leg or an arm, he cannot feel himself a complete man; he is conscious of mutilation. Children of fourteen or fifteen, educated according to modern methods, begin to be aware of a sense of mutilation if they are not permeated with the qualities of moral judgment and religious feeling. Something seems lacking in their manhood. There is no better heritage in the moral and religious sense than to bring children up to regard the elements of morality and religion as such an integral part of their being that they do not feel themselves wholly man if they are not permeated with morality, warmed through and through by religion.

This can only be achieved if we work, at the proper age, on the life of feeling and perceptive experience alone, and do not prematurely give the children intellectual conceptions of religion and morality. If we do so before the twelfth or fourteenth year, we are bringing children up to be skeptics, men and women who, instead of healthy insight, in later life develop skepticism in regard to the dogmas inculcated into them—skepticism in thought (the least important), but then skepticism in feeling, which makes them defective in feeling. And finally there will be skepticism of will which brings moral error in its train. The point is this: Our children will be brought up only to be skeptics if we present moral and religious ideals to them dogmatically; such ideals should only come to them through the life of feeling. Then, at the right age they will awaken their own free sense of religion and morality which will then become part of their very being. And they feel that only this can make them fully man. The great aim at the Waldorf school is to bring up free human beings who know how to direct their own lives.

A Modern Art of Education.
London: Rudolf Steiner Press, 1972.

Activating the Intellect

But it is also apparent today that what I have learned has absolutely no significance with regard to what kind of teacher I am for the child up to the change of teeth. After the change of teeth, it does begin to have a certain significance, but this is again lost if I impart what I have learned to the child in the form in which I bear it within me. It must all be artistically transformed, brought into pictures, as we shall see later. I must awaken imponderable forces between the child and myself. And in the second life period, from the change of teeth to puberty, what is of far greater importance than the content of what I have learned and carry in my head is whether I can transform into visual imagery, into living forms, what I unfold before the child and have to let flow into him. What a man has himself learned has significance only for children who are between puberty and the beginning of the twentieth year. For the little child up to the change of teeth the most important thing in education is the man himself. The most important element in the education of the child from the change of teeth to puberty is the human being who passes over into living artistry. Only when he has reached the age of fourteen or fifteen does the child make claims in his education and instruction upon what the teacher himself has learned. And this goes on until after the twentieth or twenty-first year, when the child is fully grown (true, we call him a young lady or young gentleman even before this) and when at twenty years he can confront another human being on equal terms, although the latter may be older.

In discussing the true method of teaching and the life conditions of education, we must speak of that enthusiasm which can be stimulated not by theoretical, abstract insight, but by real insight into the world. When we, thus, approach the child between the change of teeth and puberty, we are able to guide him/her in the right way to puberty. The moment when puberty sets in, the astral body begins to unfold its independence. What has been taken in as the music of the world goes on developing in the inner being. And the remarkable thing is that what has been developed in pictures between the change of teeth and puberty, and has become the possession of the soul in an inwardly musical, plastic sense, in living pictures, is then laid hold of by the intellect. The intellect of the human being does not take in anything at all that we force upon him intellectually from outside; his intellect takes in what has first developed within him in another way. And then this important factor comes into play: the human being has prepared what lies before the age of puberty in healthy development; he has prepared for the intelligent understanding of what he already possesses. All that he has taken hold of in pictures rises up intelligibly from his own inner wellsprings. The human being is looking into himself as he passes over to intellectual activity. He is laying hold of his own being within himself, through himself. The astral body with its musical activity beats in time with the etheric body which works plastically. There is a pulsing together within the human being, and as a result of this he becomes aware of his own being after puberty in a healthy way. And when there is this concordance between the two sides of his nature, the human being after puberty comes to a true inner experience of freedom, the result of understanding for the first time what was only perception in earlier life. The greatest thing for which we can prepare the child is that, at the right moment of life, he experiences freedom through the understanding of his own being. True freedom is an inner experience, and true freedom can only be developed when the human being is conceived of in this way. As a teacher, I must say to myself: I cannot impart freedom to the human being; he must experience it for himself. But what I have to do is to plant within him something to which his own being—this I leave untouched—feels attracted and into which it sinks itself. This is the wonderful thing I have achieved. I have educated in the human being what has to be educated. In reverence of the Godhead in every single human being, I have left untouched those things that may only be laid hold of by himself. I educate everything in the human being except what belongs to himself, and then wait for his own being to lay hold of what I have brought forth within him. I do not lay brutal hands on the development of the human self, but prepare the soil for the development of that self that sets in after puberty. If I give an overly intellectual education before puberty, if I offer abstract concepts or ready-made, sharply-outlined observations and not growing, living pictures, I am doing violence to the human being, I am laying brutal hands upon the self within him. I only educate him truly if I leave the self untouched and wait until it can take hold of what I have prepared in education. And thus, together with the child, I look forward to the time when I am able to say: Here the self is being born in its freedom; all I have done is to prepare the ground so that the self may become conscious of its own being. And if I have educated the child in this way up to puberty, I find before me a human being who says: "While I was not yet fully man, you gave me something that enables me now, when it is possible, to become fully man myself." That is to say, I have educated in such a way that with every look, every movement, the human being says to me: "You have accomplished something with me; but my freedom has been left unimpaired. You have made it possible for me to give myself my own freedom at the right moment of life. You have done something that enables me to stand before you now, shaping myself as man from out of my individuality, which you left reverently untouched."

The intellect only becomes active in its own way when the child has already reach puberty. For this reason I have already indicated that it is really a question of bringing the human being to that point where she can find in herself what she has to understand, where she can draw out of her own inner being what has been given her first for natural imitation, and then for artistic, imaginative activity. So that even in the later period we should not force things upon the human being in such a way that she feels a logical compulsion, whether she likes it or not.

It was certainly a great moment in the development of German spiritual life when, just in reference to moral experience, Schiller set himself in opposition to Kant's conception of morality. For when Kant spoke the words, "Duty, thou sublime and mighty name, thou that bearest no enticements but demandest stern submission," Schiller set himself up in opposition. He opposed this idea of duty which did not allow the moral to proceed out of the source of goodwill, but out of subjection. Schiller replied to the Kantian idea of duty in remarkable words containing a true moral motif. He said, "Willingly I serve my friend, but unfortunately I serve him from inclination; therefore, alas, I am not virtuous!" In effect, only when duty begins to be an innermost human inclination, when it becomes what Goethe expressed in the words, "Duty—where a man loves that which he tells himself to do,"—only then will the whole of the moral life proceed from human nature in its purity. It was a great moment when morality was purged of Kant's influence and made human again through Schiller and Goethe.

What came forth at that time from German spiritual life has been immersed, however, in the materialism of the

150

nineteenth century, and is still so today. We must again raise mankind out of what has arisen in civilization as a result of the fact that men have forgotten this mighty deed in the sphere of the moral. This rehabilitation of man as a fully human and moral being is the special task of those who have to teach and educate.

The Essentials of Education.
London: Rudolf Steiner Press, 1968.

Finding Anchorage in Life

If you wish to understand the whole human being you must also realize that the freeing of the body from soul and spirit in the grown man, as against the unity of body, soul, and spirit in the child, is not an abstract theory but a matter of concrete knowledge, for it protracts the time when various influences take effect in a man's life. The time that the body takes to work anything out becomes longer and longer compared with the time taken by the soul. The physical body remains behind, and harmful influences are manifested much later in the body than in the soul. So one can often see that if one transgresses against a little child in his very early years, then many wrong things will show themselves in his soul-life when he is a teenager. But this can be made good. It is not so difficult to find means of helping even apparently ungovernable children in their teens. They may even become quite good and respectable citizens later on. That is not so serious. But the body develops more and more slowly as life goes on, and the end of it all will be that long after all the soul difficulties of early youth have been overcome, the physical effects will gradually emerge, and in later life the man will have to contend with gout and other illnesses.

Then the child reaches puberty, and an important change comes about. The more general feelings of sympathy and antipathy give place to individualized feelings. Each single thing has or has not value in his eyes, but in a different way from before. This is because at puberty the real destiny of man begins to be felt. Before this time the child had more general feelings about life and looked upon it as an old acquaintance. But now, when he has attained sex-maturity, he feels that the single experiences which come to him are connected with his destiny. It is only when man conceives of life in terms of destiny that it becomes his own individual life in the right way—so what man has experienced before must be recalled a second time in order to connect it with his destiny. Before fourteen everything must be based on the authority of the teacher, but in order that it may become a part of the child's destiny, it must be presented to him again after fourteen and experienced in an individual way. This must not be left out of account. And with regard to moral concepts, we must bring the child before puberty to have such a liking for the good and such a dislike of the bad that when, in the next period of life, what he has formerly developed in sympathy and antipathy appears again in his soul, he will of himself make what he loved into his precepts and what was repugnant to him he must now eschew. This is freedom, but man can only find it if, before he comes to the "Thou shalt" and "Thou shalt not," he feels attracted to the good and repelled by the bad. It is through feeling that the child must learn morality.

With regard to religion, we must be clear that a young child is by nature religious. At the change of teeth, when the soul and spirit become freer of the body, this close connection with nature falls away, and, therefore, what was formerly natural religion has to be raised into a religion of the soul. And it is only after puberty that religious understanding can arise. Then, when the spirit has become free, what was formerly expressed in the imitation of father or mother must be handed over to the invisible, supersensible powers. Thus, there develops gradually in the child in a concrete way what has always been there in him as a germ, a seed. Nothing is grafted on to the child. It comes out of his own being.

It is really impossible to teach at all without this inward cooperation on the part of the child. In all education we must constantly be thinking of how the child will be able to go out into life at puberty. Of course, there are also the "young ladies" and "young gentlemen" who continue with their education, and in the Waldorf school we go on to University standard; we have twelve classes and take them on to their eighteenth or nineteenth year and even further. But even with these children we must realize that after puberty they do really "go out into life," and our relationship to them is quite different from what it was before. We must strive to educate in such a way that the intellect, which awakens at puberty, can then find its nourishment in the child's own nature. If during his early school years he has stored up an inner treasury of riches through imitation, through his feeling for authority, and from the pictorial character of his teaching, then at puberty these inner riches can be transmuted into intellectual activity. He will now always be faced with the task of thinking what before he has willed and felt. And we must take the very greatest care that this intellectual thinking does not appear too early. For a human being can only come to an experience of freedom if his intellectuality awakens within him of itself, not if it has been poured into him by his teachers. But it must not awaken in poverty of soul. If he has nothing within him that he has acquired through imitation and imagery, which can rise up into his thinking out of the depths of his soul, then, when his thinking should develop at puberty, he will find nothing within himself to further his own growth, and his thinking can only reach out into emptiness. He will find no anchorage in life, and just at the time when he ought really to have found a certain security in himself, he will be running after trivialities; in these awkward years of adolescence he will be imitating all kinds of things which please him (usually they are not just the things which please his elders who have a more utilitarian point of view), and he imitates these things now because he has not been allowed to imitate rightly as a young child in a living way. So it is that we may see many young people after puberty seeking a support in this or that, and thereby deadening their inner experience of freedom.

The Roots of Education.
London: Rudolf Steiner Press, 1982.

The Third Seven-Year Period

Next comes the period immediately following puberty, the period between the onset of puberty and the twenty-first or twenty-second year. Just think of all that a human being reveals to us in this phase of his life! Even with our ordinary consciousness we see evidence of a complete change in his life, but it takes a crude form. We speak of the raging hormone years, of the "awkward" years, and this in itself indicates our awareness that a change is taking place. What is actually happening is that the inner being is now emerging more clearly. But if we can acquire sensitive perception of the first two life-periods, what emerges after puberty will appear as a "second man," actually as a second man who becomes visible through the physical man standing there before us. And what expresses itself in the awkwardness, and also very much in what is admirable, appears like a second, cloud-like man within the physical man. It is important to detect this second, shadowy being, for questions on the subject are being asked on all sides today. But our civilization gives no answer.

Karmic Relationships.
London: Rudolf Steiner Press, 1957.

Understanding

But let us add something else. I said that between the change of teeth and puberty children should not be given moral precepts, but in the place of these care should be taken to ensure that what is good pleases them, because it pleases their teacher, and what is bad displeases them, because it displeases their teacher. During the second period of life everything should be built up on sympathy with the good, antipathy for the bad. Then moral feelings are implanted deeply in the soul, and there is established a sense of moral well-being in experiencing what is good and a sense of moral discomfort in experiencing what is bad. Now comes the time of puberty. Just as walking is fully developed during the first seven years, speech during the second seven years, so during the third seven years of life thinking comes fully into its own. It becomes independent. This only takes place with the oncoming of puberty; only then are we really capable of forming a judgment. If, at this time, when we begin to form thoughts out of an inner urge, feelings have already been implanted in us in the way I have indicated, then a good foundation has been laid, and we are able to form judgments. For instance, this pleases me, and I am in duty bound to act in accordance with it; that displeases me, and it is my duty to leave it alone. The significance of this is that duty itself grows out of pleasure and displeasure; it is not instilled into me but grows out of pleasure and displeasure. This is the awakening of true freedom in the human soul. We experience freedom through the fact that the sense for what is moral is the deepest individual impulse of the individual human soul. If a child has been led to a sense of the moral by an authority which is self-understood, so that the moral lives for him in the world of feeling, then after puberty the conception of duty works out of his individual inner human being. This is a healthy procedure. In this way we lead the children rightly to the point at which they are able to experience what individual freedom is. Why do people not have this experience today? They do not have it because they cannot have it, because before puberty a knowledge of good and bad was instilled into them; what they should and should not do was inculcated. But moral instruction which pays no heed to a right approach by gradual stages dries up the human being, makes out of him, as it were, a skeleton of moral precepts on which the conduct of life is hung like clothes on a coat-hanger.

The Waldorf teacher also attends meetings where the world conception of anthroposophy is studied. There he hears from those who have already acquired the necessary knowledge derived from Initiation Wisdom about such things as the following: The human being consists of physical body, etheric body, astral body, and ego. Between the seventh and fourteenth years the etheric body works mainly on the physical body; the astral body descends into the physical and etheric bodies at the time of puberty. But anyone able to penetrate deeply into these matters, anyone able to perceive more than just physical processes, whose perceptions always include spiritual processes and, when the two are separated, can perceive each separately, such a man or woman can discern how in an eleven- or twelve-year-old boy the astral body is already sounding, chiming, as it were, with the deeper tone which will first make itself heard outwardly at puberty. And a similar process takes place in the astral body of an eleven- or twelve-year-old girl.

Just as the ether body works at freeing itself in order to become independent at the time of the change of teeth, so does the astral body work in order to become independent at puberty. The ether body is a sculptor, the astral body a musician. Its structure is of the very essence of music. What proceeds from the astral body of man and is projected into form is purely musical in its nature. Anyone able to grasp this knows that in order to understand the human being a further stage of training must develop receptivity towards an inner musical conception of the world. Those who are unmusical understand nothing whatever about the formation of the astral body in man, for it is fashioned out of music. If, therefore, we study old epochs of culture which were still built up out of inner musical intuition, if we enter into such oriental epochs of culture in which even language was imbued with music, then we shall find a musical conception of the world entering even into the forms of architecture. Later on, in Greece, it became otherwise, and now, especially in the West, it has become very different, for we have entered an age when emphasis is laid on the mechanical and mathematical. In the Goetheanum at Dornach an attempt was made to go back again in this respect. Musicians have sensed the music underlying the forms of the Goetheanum. But generally speaking there is little understanding for such things today.

It is, therefore, necessary that we should gain in this way a concrete understanding of the human being and reach the point at which we are able to grasp the fact that man's physiological and anatomical form is a musical creation insofar as it stems from the astral body. Think how intimately a musical element is connected with the processes of breathing and the circulation of the blood. Man is a musical instrument in respect of his breathing and blood circulation. And if you take the relationship between the circulation of the blood and the breathing, 72 pulse beats in a minute, 18 breaths in a minute, you get a ratio of 4:1. Of course this varies individually in many ways, but by and large you find that man has an inner musical structure. The ratio 4:1 is the expression of something which, in itself an inner rhythmical relationship, nevertheless impinges on and affects the whole organization in which man lives and experiences his own being. In olden times the scansion of verses was so regulated that the line was regulated by the breath and the metrical foot by the circulation. Dactyl, dactyl, caesura, dactyl, dactyl. Four in one, the line expressive of the man.

But what man expresses in language is expressed still in education. We have no wish to introduce anthroposophy into the school, for we are no sect; what we are concerned with is universally human. We cannot, however, prevent children from leaving the evangelical and Catholic religion lessons and coming to the free religion lesson. It is not our fault, but they come. And so we have ever and again to see to it that this free religion lesson is continued.

The Waldorf school is growing, step by step. It now has about 800 children and between 40 and 50 teachers. Its growth is well in hand—not so its finances. The financial situation is very precarious. Less than six weeks ago there was no means of knowing whether the financial position would allow the Waldorf school to exist beyond June 15th. Here we have an example which shows clearly how difficult it is today for an undertaking to hold its own in the face of the terrible state of economic affairs in Central Europe, even though it has proved beyond any manner of doubt the spiritual justification for its existence. Again and again, every month, we experience the utmost anxiety as to how we are to make the existence of the Waldorf school economically possible. Destiny allows us to work, but in such a way that the Sword of Damocles—financial need—is always hanging over our heads. As a matter of principle we must continue to work, as if the Waldorf school were established for eternity. This certainly demands a very pronounced devotion on the part of the teaching staff, who work with inner intensity without any chance of knowing whether in three months' time they will be unemployed.

Nevertheless, Waldorf education has grown out of anthroposophy. What has been least sought for is what prospers best. In other words, what the gods have given, not what men have made, is most blessed with good fortune. It is quite comprehensible that the art of education is something which perforce lies especially close to the hearts of anthroposophists. For what is really the most inwardly beautiful thing in the world? Surely it is the growing, developing human being. To see this human being from the spiritual world enter into the physical world through birth, to observe how what lives in him, what he has carried down in definite form, is gradually becoming more and more defined in his features and movements, to behold in the right way divine forces, divine manifestations working through the human form into the physical world—all this has something about it which in the deepest sense we may call religious. No wonder, therefore, that wherever there is the striving towards the purest, truest, most intimate humanity, such a striving as exists as the very foundation of anything anthroposophical, one contemplates the riddle of the growing human being with sacred, religious fervor and brings towards it all the work of which one is capable.

That is something which, arising out of the deepest impulses of the soul, calls forth within the anthroposophical movement enthusiasm for the art of education. So one may truly say: The art of education stands within the anthroposophical movement as a creation which can be nurtured in no other way than with love. It is so nurtured. It is indeed nurtured with the most devoted love. And so many venture to say further that the Waldorf school is taken to the heart of all who know it and what thrives there, thrives in a way that must be looked upon as an inner necessity.

Human Values in Education.
London: Rudolf Steiner Press, 1971.

Gender Observations

The child is curious, but not with an intellectual curiosity, for as yet it has no reasoning powers, and anyone who appeals to the intellect of a child of seven is quite on the wrong lines; but it has fantasy, and it is this with which we must deal. It is really a question of developing the concept of a kind of "milk of the soul." For you see, after birth the child must be given bodily milk. This constitutes her food, and every other necessary substance is contained in the milk that the child consumes. And when she comes to school at the age of the changing of the teeth, it is again milk that you must give her, but now, milk for the soul. That is to say, your teaching must not be made up of isolated units, but all that the child receives must be a unity; when she has gone through the change of teeth she must have "soul milk." If she is taught to read and write as two separate things, it is just as though her milk were to be separated chemically into two different parts, and you gave her one part at one time and the other at another. Reading and writing must form a unity. You must bring this idea of "soul milk" into being for your work with the children when they first come to school.

This can only come about if, after the change of teeth, the children's education is directed artistically. The artistic element must be in it all. Tomorrow I will describe more fully how to develop writing out of painting and thus give it an artistic form, and how you must then lead this over artistically to the teaching of reading, and how this artistic treatment of reading and writing must be connected, again by artistic means, with the first simple beginnings of arithmetic. All this must thus form a unity. Such things as these must be gradually developed as "soul milk" which we need for the child when he comes to school.

And when he reaches the age of puberty, he will require "spiritual milk." This is extremely difficult to give to present-day humanity, for we have no spirit left in our materialistic age. It will be a difficult task to create "spiritual milk," but if we cannot succeed in creating it, we shall have to leave our boys and girls to themselves at the so-called "raging hormone" stage, for there is no "spiritual milk" in our present age.

Man consists not only of his physical body and etheric body, which later is emancipated and free at the seventh year, but also of the astral body and ego. What happens to the astral body of the child between the seventh and fourteenth years? It does not really come to its full activity until puberty. Only then is it working completely within the human organism. But while the etheric body between birth and the change of teeth is in a certain sense being drawn out of the physical body and becoming independent, the astral body is gradually being drawn inwards between the seventh and fourteenth years, and when it has been drawn right in and is no longer merely loosely connected with the physical and etheric bodies but permeates them completely, then the human being has arrived at the moment of puberty, of sex maturity.

With the boy one can see by the change of voice that the astral body is now quite within the larynx; with the girl one can see by the development of other organs, breast organs, and so on, that the astral body has now been completely drawn in. The astral body finds its way slowly into the human body from all sides.

The lines and directions it follows are the nerve fibers. The astral body comes in along the nerve fibers from without inwards. Here it begins to fill out the whole body from the outer environment, from the skin, and gradually draws itself together inside. Before this time it is a kind of loose cloud in which the child lives. Then it draws itself together, lays firm hold upon all the organs, if we may put it somewhat crudely, it unites itself chemically with the organism, with all the tissues of the physical and etheric bodies.

But something very strange happens here. When the astral body presses inwards from the periphery of the body, it makes its way along the nerves which then unite in the spine. Above is the head. It also forces its way slowly through the head nerves, crawls along the nerves towards the central organs, towards the spinal cord, bit by bit, into the head, gradually coming in and filling it all out.

The Kingdom of Childhood.
London: Rudolf Steiner Press, 1964.

Bibliography

Steiner, Rudolf. *A Modern Art of Education,* Ilkley, August 5-17, 1923, Rudolf Steiner Press, 1972.

_____. *A Social Basis for Education,* Stuttgart, November 5,1919 and January 6,1919, Steiner Schools Fellowship.

_____. *After the Fourteenth Year,* Steiner Schools Fellowship.

_____. *Anthroposophically Based Education and Teaching Methods,* Two lectures, Oslo, November 23, 24, 1921, 2nd lecture. Translated by Christiana Bryan, October 15, 1955, Rudolf Steiner Press.

_____. *At the Gates of Spiritual Science,* Stuttgart, August 27, 1906, Rudolf Steiner Press. Now published as *The Education of the Child and Early Lectures on Education,* Anthroposophic Press, 1996.

_____. *Education as a Social Problem,* Dornach, August 9, 1919 and August 17, 1919, Anthroposophic Press.

_____. *Human Values in Education,* Arnhem, July 1924, Rudolf Steiner Press, 1971, Anthroposophic Press, 1995.

_____. *Karmic Relationships,* Vol. VII Lecture 6, Breslaw, December 6, 1924, Rudolf Steiner Press.

_____. *Meditatively Acquired Knowledge of Man,* September 1920, Stuttgart, Steiner Schools Fellowship. Now published as *Balance in Teaching,* Mercury Press, 1982.

_____. *Practical Advice to Teachers,* Rudolf Steiner Press, 1976, Anthroposophic Press, 2000.

_____. *Soul Economy and Waldorf Education,* Oslo, November 1921, Anthroposophic Press/Rudolf Steiner Press, 1986.

_____. *Spiritual Ground of Education,* Oxford, August 1922, Rudolf Steiner Press.

_____. *Study of Man*, August/September 1919, Stuttgart, Rudolf Steiner Press, 1966. Now published as *Foundations of Human Experience*, Anthroposophic Press, 1996.

_____. *Supplementary Course*, Stuttgart, June 1921, Steiner Schools Fellowship/Kolisko. Now published as *Education for Adolescents*, Anthroposophic Press, 1996.

_____. *The Child's Changing Consciousness and Waldorf Education*, Dornach, April 1923, Rudolf Steiner Press, 1988. Now published as *The Child's Changing Consciousness as the Basis of Pedagogical Practice*, Anthroposophic Press, 1996.

_____. *The Education of the Child in the Light of Anthroposophy*, Rudolf Steiner Press, 1965.

_____. *The Essentials of Education*, Stuttgart, April 8-12, 1924, Rudolf Steiner Press, 1968, Anthroposophic Press, 1997.

_____. *The Kingdom of Childhood*, Torquay, August 1924, Anthroposophic Press, 1995.

_____. *The Renewal of Education*, Dornach, April/May 1920, Steiner Schools Fellowship/Kolisko.

_____. *The Roots of Education*, Bern, April 1924, Rudolf Steiner Press, 1982, Anthroposophic Press, 1998.

_____. *The Younger Generation*, Stuttgart, October 1922, Anthroposophic Press, 1967.

Note:

All excerpts indicating the Anthroposophic Press were used by permission of

Anthroposophic Press,
PO Box 960,
Herndon, VA 20172-0960

All excerpts indicating the Rudolf Steiner Press were used by permission of the

Rudolf Steiner Press,
51 Queen Caroline Street,
London, W6 9QL Great Britain

Index

A

B

C

freed-up intelligence 44
freedom 53, 146, 149, 154
freemasonry 92-93

G

geography 61
girls 71, 72, 75-77, 86, 97, 107-111, 130, 140, 142, 160
Goethe 95, 124, 150
goodness 105, 123
grammar 59, 62
gratitude 102, 118, 123
Greco-Latin culture 54
Greek 57, 72-73, 81, 126, 138-139
Gymnast, importance of 138

H

Haeckel, Ernst 104
Hamerling, Robert 127
handicraft 49, 124
handwork 79
head system 41
health 113
healthy logic 124
healthy thinking 124
heredity 16
history 97
Holy Grail 32-34
Homer 96
human judgment 50
human love 45
human thought 60
human voice 90

I

J

K

N

O

P

R

S

T